ARCHIZINES
ARCHIZINES
ARCHIZINES
ARCHIZINES
ARCHIZINES
ARCHIZINES
ARCHIZINES
ARCHIZINES
ARCHIZINES
ARCHIZINES

EDITED BY
ELIAS REDSTONE

ZINES

BEDFORD PRESS, LONDON

CHITECTURAL

ELIAS REDSTONE

ON ARCHIZINES

COLLECTING (A BRIEF HISTORY)

Exhibitions have to start somewhere, and in this case it began with a personal interest. About five years ago I became aware of, and started collecting, fanzines about architecture. Thanks to publishing fairs such as Publish & Be Damned, and a few well-stocked independent bookshops in London, I was discovering titles that were made by people who were obsessed with a place or a certain building and wanted to share their enthusiasm.

In 2006 I was introduced to Felix Burrichter. He had a black-and-white print-out of a new magazine he was making called *PIN-UP*. Felix was passionate about creating a magazine that was about architecture, but intelligent and sexy at the same time. When *PIN-UP*'s inaugural issue was published that autumn it didn't just look fantastic, it was something I wanted to read. Although the weekly and monthly publications that landed on my desk were informative, here someone my age had created something I could really connect with. An independent spirit could work just as well in a photocopied fanzine as in a more conventional magazine format. It was a moment when I felt that things were starting to get exciting.

In 2008 I was awarded funding from the Winston Churchill Memorial Trust to research contemporary architecture in Latin America. In each country I visited, architects were publishing magazines – *SPAM* and *Public Library* in Chile; *UR* and *PLOT* in Argentina to name a few – but this was not some connected network of editors or online community. Here were individuals or collectives that wanted to have a voice: people who were not catered for by the conventional press. At the same time, student journals at architecture schools were being launched while forgotten titles were revived and refreshed.

Back in Europe, more publications started to appear. Between 2008 and 2010 six new titles launched in the UK alone: *Block*, *Civic City Cahier*, *P.E.A.R.*, *Preston is my Paris*, *matzine* and *Touching on Architecture*. Despite the dominance of the internet, there was clearly a desire by many to express themselves in print. And it was happening everywhere. In different countries and different settings people were using the resources they could activate to print opinions, ideas, proposals, photography and a whole assortment of other content.

With every international trip the collection grew. Soon I was filling a box with architecture publications that I marked 'ARCHIZINES' – a word blended from architecture and magazine as a way of grouping the various types of publications. While there have been projects to consider previous generations of architectural publishing – Clip Stamp Fold, for example, expertly explored the output of the 1960s and 1970s – I wanted to do something to celebrate and promote the creative material that was being produced today. It became apparent that there was an exhibition here waiting to happen.

EXPANDING

Rather perversely for a project that fetishises printed matter, it made sense for ARCHIZINES to start life online. While I was still learning about this emerging publishing phenomenon, a website allowed me to catalogue publications systematically as I uploaded them, to showcase the publications, to reach out to other titles I had not yet come across and to edit and refine the project as it grew.

With a shared interest in print, Folch Studio came on board to create an identity and brand the website. In January 2011 the website went live and I systematically went through the publications in my collection to archive them online – photographing spreads, writing introductions, uploading basic statistics – to create an online showcase of new publishing and promote the work to a wide audience.

Knowledge is always limited. Although I have scoured bookshops and websites for interesting publications, I knew I was barely aware of a fraction of what was out there. I needed to know more. So to get the word out I emailed some journalists and bloggers and, thanks to abitare, archdaily, deconcrete, dezeen, manystuff and other sites, the word got out. Thousands of people started visiting the website. I started a Facebook page. Within a few days it was 'liked' by more people than I actually know friends, and after a couple of months it had 1,000 fans.

Then suddenly I started receiving emails from people all over the world who were editing their own publications, asking if they could show me their work. Packages began arriving from the USA, Canada, Australia, China and countries across Europe. With so many publications piling up, it became time to actually define what I meant by an ARCHIZINE.

DEFINING

ARCHIZINES was set up to showcase new architecture magazines, fanzines and journals that provide an alternative to the established architectural press. 'Alternative' is a relative concept and is necessarily subjective. There is no scientific rule as to what should be showcased, but some guidelines were introduced.

It is important that the publication is a periodical – producing more than one issue – or a publishing outfit with a number of one-off titles like *Public Library* or *no now*. While there have been some interesting one-off projects, an ongoing commitment to the cause is necessary here.

ARCHIZINES set out to survey what is happening now. This meant that the publication had to have been launched after 2000. It was an arbitrary date, but a decade felt right for this project. Indeed, most of the titles were launched after 2005 and many only in the last year or two. There are some titles that have consistently published interesting independent projects for much longer – *Circo* and *Pamphlet Architecture* to name just two – but a line had to be drawn. Other titles that have been in existence for many years but have radically reinvented themselves within the last decade have been included.

The publications come from all over the world (over 20 countries at the last count) and are published by many people (architects, artists, academics, students and others). They vary in style (from photocopied zines to professionally printed and bound magazines) and content (from architectural research to personal narratives and writing about buildings and cities). So a publication that reinterprets the aesthetics of an architecture magazine sits beside a hand-stitched pamphlet containing experimental text. Circulation figures range from 30 to 25,000. Some are distributed widely, others are not available outside the country where they are produced. What they share in common is an interest in documenting and discussing the spaces we occupy in ways not found in existing mainstream or professional publications.

EXHIBITING

In November 2010 I sent a proposal to the exhibitions team at the Architectural Association and they expressed interest in hosting an exhibition. Curating the ARCHIZINES exhibition brought its own set of challenges. *What is being exhibited? Do we need vitrines to protect the manuscripts? How does it become a spatial experience?*

From the start, it was important that visitors should be able to handle the publications and browse through them at leisure. They should find out what makes them interesting, what they feel like and where they come from. It was decided that each publication would show one issue – not necessarily the newest or the first, but the editors could pick an issue that was important to them or representative of the publication in some way. The exhibition space allowed for 60 publications to be displayed.

At the same time, I wanted the exhibition to be an opportunity to bring the international community together. This was achieved via film. All the editors were asked to record themselves answering four open questions: *What is the relationship between architecture and publishing? How do you 'edit' architecture? What is the role of printed matter in the digital age? How are architectural publications changing?* The cumulative answers give an insight into current thinking on these topics as well as revealing something of the personalities behind the publications.

This catalogue is also a space to explore further the relationship between architecture and publishing. Themes addressed in the essays include the role of publishing in academia and architectural practice, and the representation of architecture in fictional writing, photography, magazines and fanzine culture. There are immediate questions that the project raises – *Why are people printing all these architecture publications now? What is their importance?* – which the essays in this catalogue move towards answering. However, this whole project should stimulate and provoke more questions, discussion and research, along with new publishing experiments. It will only be with time that the impact of these ARCHIZINES on architecture, culture and publishing will be understood.

ENDING

I am not sure what the future holds for the publications showcased here. Some will flourish, others may cease publishing, and yet more will appear. Funding is probably the single biggest challenge facing this type of publishing and only a few exist as commercial ventures. Grants for cultural activities are almost universally being squeezed. The Netherlands, previously an advocate for this sector, is threatening to withdraw public funding for architecture magazines arguing that they should be considered commercial, not cultural, publications.

This publication captures a snapshot of activity taking place in the world right now. It is by no means a comprehensive survey as every week more titles are launched or make themselves known. I have just found out about the first architecture magazine launching in East Africa, from the team behind *Camenzind*, and a new fanzine published in Norway. As I am writing this, an email arrived from an architect editing a journal in Estonia.

The ARCHIZINES exhibition and catalogue mark a moment in time, but it does not stop here. The exhibition will tour internationally and new publications will be added along the way. All the publications collected in this research project will be transferred to the National Art Library at the Victoria & Albert Museum. By providing a permanent home for these publications, this period of publishing activity will be available as a public resource for generations to come.

If anything, this is a beginning and not an ending.

AMERICA DESERTA REVISITED

London, UK
www.tomkeeley.co.uk

America Deserta Revisited is the latest self-publishing project from artist Tom Keeley, a co-founder of the Sheffield-based fanzine *Go* that ran from 2004 to 2008. The series of five titles is the result of a trip by train across the USA, and is consid-ered by the author as a 'series of urban guidebooks to the soul, rather than the sights of a place'. It is a response to Reyner Banham's touristic approach to exploring the state of the union in the US, and examines the key urban issues the country faces as the oil gradually runs out. The five fanzines in the series are available as a boxset.

America Deserta Revisited 3: Detroit, October 2011

ANOTHER PAMPHLET

New York City, USA
www.anotherpamphlet.com

another pamphlet was launched by Isaiah King, Ryan Neiheiser and Giancarlo Valle in 2011 as 'a conversation, a loose exchange of forms and ideas, an excuse to play, a frame through which to look, a shared excitement. It is an open dialogue with our friends, our histories, and our surroundings.' Each submission is limited to 300 words and one image. The A5 zine is self-printed and distributed by post. 'Against the haze of digital distraction, we crave an object to hold our attention – something to touch, to fold, to tuck in our back pocket, to discard'. Six issues will be produced each year.

another pamphlet 2: Repetition!, August 2011
140 × 216 mm; 20 pages; 400 copies

APARTAMENTO

Barcelona, Spain
www.apartamentomagazine.com

Apartamento features photography, essays and discussions about the spaces people occupy. The first issue was launched in April 2008 as a 'magazine interested in homes, living spaces and design solutions as opposed to houses, photo ops and design dictatorships'. As well as publishing the magazine twice a year, directors Nacho Alegre and Omar Sosa and editor-in-chief Marco Velardi create projects and events at the Salone de Mobile in Milan, London Design Festivals and other cities.

Apartamento 7, April 2011; 170 × 240 mm; 226 pages; 22,000 copies

ARCHINECT NEWS DIGEST

Los Angeles, USA
www.archinect.com

Archinect News Digest is a publication that culls content from Archinect.com and redistributes it into themed and curated issues of 'immediate and pressing interest'. A collaboration between Archinect.com and Friction House Publishing, the first issue focuses on the artist, architect and activist Ai Wei Wei. According to the editors Christian Chaudhari and Paul Petrunia, 'super compressed one-week production time makes the magazine hyper responsive and gives it a rough and energetic styling'.

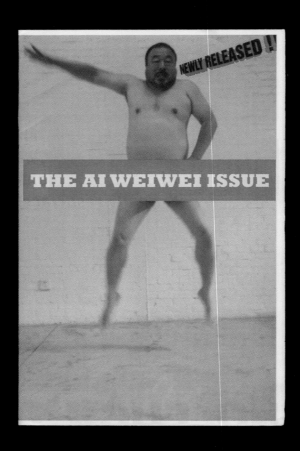

THE AI WEIWEI ISSUE

NEWLY RELEASED !!

Archinect News Digest 1: The Ai Weiwei Issue, July 2011
140 × 216 mm, 30 pages; 100 copies

BEYOND

Amsterdam, Netherlands
www.sunarchitecture.nl

Beyond, Short Stories on the Post-Contemporary is dedicated to new, experimental forms of architectural and urban writing. Conceived by editor-in-chief Pedro Gadanho as a 'bookzine', it includes contributions from an extended network of young and upcoming European architectural writers who are given the freedom to survey the out-

line of themes and things to come. 'The first issue set the series' agenda of focusing on the near future. While subsequent themes were broader in philosophical implications, *Scenarios and Speculations* addressed the way in which fiction and other experimental forms of architectural writing can help us envisage and reflect upon possibilities for architecture and the coming city'. The first three issues were published by SUN Architecture.

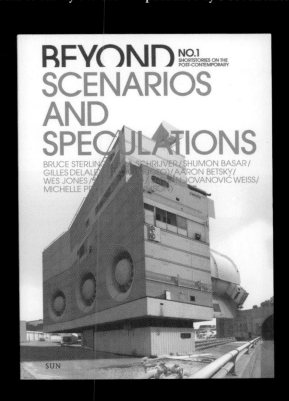

Beyond, Short Stories on the Post-Contemporary 1: Scenarios and Speculations, April 2009; 170 x 240 mm; 120 pages; 1,500 copies

BLOCK

London, UK
www.blockmagazine.co.uk

Block is a magazine for writing – review, reflection, story, poem or polemic – on architecture, built space and the city and its representation or exploration through sketch, photograph, drawing and graphic image. Launched by Rob Wilson and Ed Wilson, and designed by Ellie and Katya Duffy, *Block* aims to present architecture's reflection across a wider field of contemporary culture, and its place within it. Each issue is themed and the content combines documentary, commentary, opinion and critique, the fictional and the imaginary. 'This launch issue feels like a statement of intent for the magazine as a whole, establishing an initial marker for its content, structure, format and feel.'

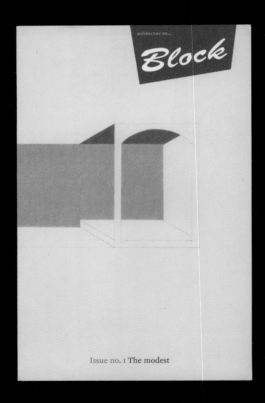

Block 1: The Modest, June 2010; 297 × 190mm; 54 pages; 1,300 copies

BRACKET

Toronto, Canada
www.brkt.org

Bracket is a new annual series structured around an open call for entries that highlights emerging critical issues at the juncture of architecture, environment and digital culture. Conceived as an almanac, the series looks at emerging thematics in our global age that are shaping the built environment in significant, yet often unexpected ways. The first issue looks at the capacity for architecture to address ideas and issues of productive landscapes and urbanisms. *Bracket* is produced as a collaboration between InfraNet Lab and Archinect, and published by Actar.

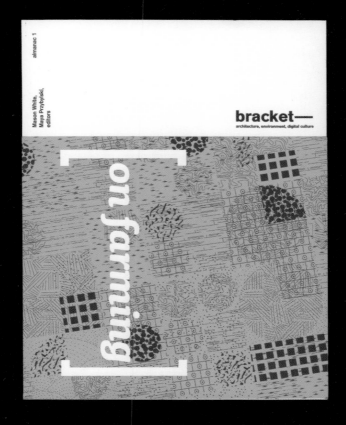

Bracket 1: On Farming, October 2010; 200 × 260 mm; 252 pages; 2,500 copies

CAMENZIND

Zurich, Switzerland
www.cazmag.com

Camenzind was founded in 2005 and positions itself in the gap between glossy magazines and professional architectural journals. The editors believe that since architecture concerns everyone, it should be discussed in an open way by a wide range of contributors. 'In our eighth issue, jokes about famous architects stand alongside serious reports about prostitution in Zurich. The satirical tone means that the reader can never be sure whether they are expected to laugh out loud or express concern... With this anarchic eclecticism we aspire to democratise the discourse and offer a new way for readers to engage with architecture and urbanism.'

Camenzind 8: The Great Report from Paradise, January 2011
130 × 185 mm; 138 pages; 400 copies

CANDIDE

Aachen, Germany
www.candidejournal.net

Candide – Journal for Architectural Knowledge was founded at the Department for Architecture Theory, RWTH Aachen University, Germany in 2009. It was inspired by Voltaire's fictional character *Candide*, who travelled the eighteenth-century world in an eager but often disappointed search for knowledge.

Edited by Axel Sowa and Susanne Schindler, each issue is made up of five distinct sections that 'respond to the diversity of architectural knowledge being produced, while challenging authors of all disciplines to test a variety of genres to write about and represent architecture'. The first three issues were published by Transcript. Issue four is the first issue to be published by Actar.

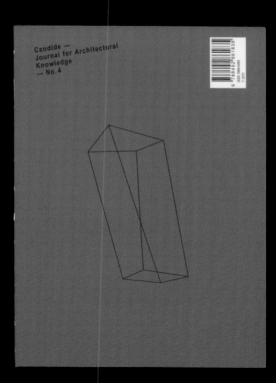

Candide —
Journal for Architectural
Knowledge
— No. 4

Candide – Journal for Architectural Knowledge 4, July 2011
170 mm × 240 mm; 136 pages; 1,500 copies

CIVIC CITY CAHIER

London, UK
www.bedfordpress.org

The *Civic City Cahier* series, launched by Jesko Fezer and Matthias Görlich in 2010, intends to provide material for a critical discussion about the role of design for a new social city. It publishes short monographic texts by authors who specialise in urban and design theory and practice. *Civic City Cahier* is published by Bedford Press, a publishing imprint of the Architectural Association that seeks to develop contemporary models of publication practice.

Civic City
Cahier 3

Tom Holert
Distributed
Agency,
Design's
Potentiality

Bedford Press

Civic City Cahier 3: Distributed Agency, Design's Potentiality
March 2011; 115 × 190 mm; 72 pages; 750 copies

ROB WILSON

ON PUBLISHING ARCHITECTURE

(EVEN THOUGH THERE'S NO CASH IN MAGS...)

... or so I was repeatedly told when I started one. It is pretty much true of course and especially so for magazines on architecture – a subject which has never at the best of times had the mass plastered-over-the-teenage-bedroom appeal of music or fashion.

Still, one suspects most of the rash of architecture magazines that have recently launched didn't necessarily have fine-tuned business plans designed to run on the *Monocle* model, let alone that of *Mojo*.

Blessed as we are to live in that old chestnut of interesting times – Lehman Brothers and all that – there is a palpable sense of change in the air: not only out-with-the-old, but a fair bit of in-with-the-new too. Yet with the dip in the construction industry, existing architecture titles have seen advertising and readership drop whilst content has leached to pay-to-view websites; and with Kindles and i-Pads now ramping up the quality of digital content, it would seem a particularly inopportune moment to dip a toe into architectural print media. Indeed you might expect the latter to be dwindling away quietly from neglect.

Yet the opposite is true, as can be seen by the variety of publications presented in ARCHIZINES. For concurrent with the economic slide and the rise of the digital, there has been an unexpected flowering of independent architectural publishing in seemingly rather barren soil. So what have been the reasons and motivations behind the spike in numbers of architecture publications in the last few years? It's obviously not the money, so why now?

36

For one, a time of winnowing always provides a new clarity, and the evident failure of the status quo to foresee, prevent or deal with the consequences of the financial crash, in the world of construction and property as much as in any other sphere, proved a salutary wake-up call for many involved in architecture, myself included, and a desire to find a way to proactively contribute to a change of culture, broadening out the debate of what architecture could or should be.

For whilst the vacuity of the super-consumerist culture that developed over the last decade or so – in which architecture and regeneration became co-opted – was something everyone was aware of and complained about, no one felt charged to change it. In any case, certainly in the UK, architecture appeared to have moved to a more central role in culture, attracting wider appreciation in public and private life: with high-profile awards, television programmes and individuals newly empowered not just to re-wallpaper but rebuild or reboot their houses, seemingly a good thing in a previously heritage-obsessed nation.

But the flipside is that architecture has risked being reduced to just an expendable consumer item in the private sphere or, alternatively, to being presented as another career-path vehicle, be it rather slow-burn, to become a celebrity or brand on the back of an iconic public building or two. Meanwhile its importance as a socially engaged art form, not a fashion statement, appears to be somewhat sidelined.

This is at least the gist of what an architect friend, Ed Wilson, and I got talking about at a café in Fez in early 2008 (distance no doubt giving perspective), a conversation that seeded the idea to launch the magazine *Block*.

In particular, I remember, we discussed the limitations and supine nature of the existing architectural media, which, between anodyne redesigns and storm-in-a-teacup headlines, had increasingly become either just a string of critically toothless PR features ('glossy archi-porn touting the unsullied flesh of freshly minted buildings', as we later dismissed it in the somewhat over-purple prose of the call for contributions to *Block*'s first issue), or conversely, narrowly academic, with articles opaque to all but specialist archi-geeks.

Whilst we didn't think at the time that we were exactly a voice crying in the wilderness, only later did it become apparent that rather a lot of similar discussions – about the glossy or opaque irrelevance of current architecture media – were going on elsewhere (witness the scope of the ARCHIZINES project), conversations fuelled, perhaps as always in a downturn, by more people having more time on their hands: time to reflect and vent frustration. But they were conversations that also turned into action in a spirit of do-it-yourself since noone else is. Thus *Apartamento* launched in early 2008, states it is 'a magazine interested in homes, living spaces and design solutions as opposed to houses, photo ops and design dictatorships... a logical result of the post-materialist mind shift. People are bored with the ostentatious and über-marketing.' *Camenzind*, rather more presciently founded in 2005, meanwhile positions itself 'between shiny interior magazines and professional architectural journals', aiming to discuss architecture 'in a way comprehensible for everybody.'

Other magazines seem to explore more positive resistance and the possibilities of architecture as a force for change. *Towards an Architecture of Opposition* promotes 'current attempts at architecture as activism'; *Megawords* promises 'to have a voice free from the noise of commercialisation'. Sometimes the tone taken is coolly critical of architecture's (ir)redeemably compromised implication in the existing order: a review of 'architecture's privileged position at the heart of the politics, society and economics, describing and examining architecture and its issues as a way to critique the world that builds it', as *Criticat* puts it; or examining as *Scapegoat* does, 'the relationship between capitalism and the built environment, confronting the coercive and violent organisation of space, the exploitation of labour and resources, and the unequal distribution of environmental risks and benefits'. Sometimes it is stridently manifesto-like: '*face b* considers architecture as a mass media; *face b* is a propaganda tool'; or sometimes just plain angry: '*Foreign Architects Switzerland* is meant as a platform for ideas, projects, and people that remain illegitimate to the brain-dead, incestuous architectural media of Switzerland.'

What is palpable though when looking at the statements of intent with which so many recent architecture magazines choose to introduce themselves, is this sense of frustration at the state of things, at the tired tropes of the existing order, and the desire to do something about it (whilst of course exercising a healthy dose of ego) and contribute to the debate by creating: 'an open-ended forum' (*Conditions*), 'a meeting place' (*Engawa*), 'a conversation / open dialogue / loose exchange' (*another pamphlet*), 'a topography of ideas' (*MAP*); each in essence 'a magazine about architecture' (*San Rocco*), and each reflecting a field of divergent views.

The DIY spirit has undoubtedly been helped to publishing reality by the technology available now – the ease and relative cheapness of digital printing. Looking back this has happened before. Indeed, whenever there has been an alignment of stars between economic bad-times and technological innovation or its new mass availability, a spike in independent architecture publishing has occurred. So in the 60s and 70s this paralleled, and drew momentum from, a new ubiquity of Gestetners and spirit duplicators (aaahh the smell of hymn-sheets in assembly!) – whilst by the early 90s, it was desktop publishing and improved, cheaper photocopying.

But this time, digital technology has not only eased the passage to print, but also to the market and potential audiences – through email, websites, blogs and tweets. And this ubiquity of missives seems to have unleashed a thirst to write.

In the 90s recession, the effect of architects and architectural students having more time on their hands resulted in a wave of experimentation using Photoshop and CAD programmes to produce a new type of paper architecture – ideas through image, presenting unbuilt projects as a new virtual practice – which questioned and reinvented what an architecture practice could be by looking at the cross-disciplinary possibilities of architecture as art, graphics or branding. Now, it appears the extension or reinvigoration of practice is often through writing.

This revival of writing and thirst to write, whetted perhaps by the blogo-sphere – of lone voices getting out to mass audiences – has seen reinvestment in the value of writing about architecture: as a form of representation, of curating, of practice, and is an outlet for imagination and creative energy. This focus on the written word in many of the new magazines is significant. *Beyond: Short Stories on the Post-Contemporary* is dedicated to 'new, experimental forms of architectural and urban writing', whilst *Log* states more explicitly it is 'a journal for new architectural writing and criticism. A carefully crafted compendium of essays, conversations (interviews), and short observations on contemporary buildings and trends, *Log* eschews the visual culture of the moment in favour of determined forays into the critical and cultural implications of the discipline.'

Block also deliberately foregrounds 'thought-provoking writing on architecture, built space and the city – review, reflection, story, poem or polemic' first, ahead of 'its exploration through sketch, photograph, drawing and graphic image', seeing writing as a key form of representation.

The sheer number of new magazines taking architecture and urbanism as their stated centre of gravity, but directed at a broader audience, is also notable.

This reflects a new confidence in and reassessment of architecture as an autonomous art form, in and of itself, both of general interest, and more comfortable in its own skin as a specialist discipline. For whilst the perception of the expanded field of architecture practice remains, there's now very little talk of 'cross-disciplinarity'.

Architecture has re-established its sense of cen-
trality as a discipline, with the cross-fertilisation
at its edges not looking out so much – as to how
architectural practice leaches into other practices
and art forms, but more at how other disciplines
reference back to architecture – witness so much
recent art practice utilising architecture as inspiration. This is reflected in publications such as
Touching on Architecture, launched in 2008, 'a step
into architecture via a critical work of a single
non-architect. Writers, artists, musicians, designers + theorists are invited to publish their current
work or research, in reflection of how these outputs touch upon architectural constructions.'
Meanwhile commentary, critique and columns
on architecture have popped up in art magazines.
This shift was something we were keen *Block*
should focus on: 'considering architecture's reflection across the wider field of contemporary culture and its place within it' by including work
from artists, writers, poets and photographers,
as well as architects and architectural historians.

 A further element in the mini architectural
publishing renaissance of today is the renewed
enjoyment of the printed page – of the 'thing-ness'
of magazines themselves. In inverse reaction
to the triumph of the digital, there's been the
perhaps inevitable blowback (familiarity breeding
contempt and all that), a thirst for print matter,
for a nice object and its non-visual sensualities of
smell, texture, weight: the exoticism of the real.
This certainly contributed to our thinking at *Block*
– we discussed the importance of the magazine
needing to be a nice thing to hold – and it seems
to have been an element in other editors' thinking

too. *another pamphlet* describes itself as 'perversely anachronistic. It will be printed on paper and distributed via – gasp – the post... Against the haze of digital distraction, we crave an object to hold our attention – something to touch, to fold, to tuck in our back pocket, to discard...' As this statement shows, producing a piece of print can be about the savouring of it as a physical object to keep, but also to throw away – as an ephemeral thing. This enjoyment of the present visceral soon-to-be-lost moment is materially different from the virtual ephemerality of the internet, with its potentially eternal moment, forever posted up somewhere.

So a printed magazine can be cast as both a Luddite taste for slow food and as a hit-the-spot take-out, distinctive from the internet's continual rolling buffet. But in either case, with great graphics remaining key for such design-centric publications, these are still superior and have more power in the hand than on the screen, however big or good its resolution.

The printed object also gives the pleasure of the contained, of a completeness in itself, of the particular edit: not the last word on a subject – which otherwise could be forever fugitively chased on the internet – but a subjective, incomplete, yet definite choice of selected, selective views; removed from the itch to endlessly scroll further out into the ether.

The remit and content of magazines such as *The Archinect News Digest* which 'culls content from Archinect.com and redistributes it into themed and curated issues of immediate and pressing interest' makes this into a positive virtue, with the aim that 'the super compressed one-week production time makes the magazine hyper-responsive and gives it a rough and energetic styling'.

Whilst the methods for the 'containment' of content is achieved through varying editorial policies in different magazines, it usually involves some structuring thematic providing the rough boundary, with contributions collated through peer review or commissioning, open submission or as a summary of recent research or practice – and everything in between.

Of course all magazines are cut differently – with a shifting balance between print and web presence, discourse, practice, image and word – and the definition of what an architecture magazine might be has widened out, sometimes naturally in direct contradiction to the generalisations I've sketched above: for instance, in *San Rocco*, 'pictures are more important than texts', and so on.

I have deliberately not touched on the issue of funding, glowering in the background. Suffice it to say, the differing models and takes on financial survival that are common are often not fully commercial, with support often coming from universities for which magazines can act as an arm of research or dissemination; and from organisations and agencies, where they can be both research and development and soft marketing; or through related events, programmes or partnerships. But the signs are, that if a magazine is good enough to generate interest and a readership, somewhere out there funding can usually be found to support it, though it may be through different means than that of the traditional subscription route.

This new wave of architecture magazines emerging and finding their voice is important. It marks a refreshing shift in how architecture is disseminated, and moves the goal-posts of architectural publishing at the same time as digital media is making its impact felt. In recognition of this changed landscape, older magazines that provided inspiration in the past, such as the *Architectural Review* (*AR*), are changing their structure and editorial agenda, restating their commitment to good critique and the value of print. Heralding their recent redesign, *AR* stated: 'print and web... (will) play to their respective strengths. The magazine's role will be reoriented towards areas where print can excel – such as longer pieces and high-quality images – with more supplementary content migrating online.' The aim of this is for the content to give 'greater depth, with longer pieces of criticism, more incisive reportage and a greater emphasis on drawings, provocative and relevant architectural discourse'.

And all this to reinvigorate *AR*'s traditional role to 'place itself at the vanguard of architectural culture and production, not as a passive observer, but as a vocal participant and speculative activist within the profession.' A good summary of the value and power of architectural magazines on which to end.

All quotes taken from the respective magazine websites.

l, Netherlands
donny.com

y is a strictly unedited
the personal experi-
ture in the urban
nt. It was established
Samira Ben Laloua,
ggeman and Ernst
even and is published
'Due to global ur-
most people consider
their natural environ-

ment. The perception
and nature has change
Club Donny we offer a
that aims to bring into
light observations, coi
stories and encounters
obvious and sometime
existence of nature in
In addition to the mag
Club Donny sees itself
where people from all
world can gather and s
images and stories.

CLUB DONNY #7

y 7, September 2011; 210 x 297 mm; 36 Pages

CONDITIONS

Oslo, Norway
www.conditionsmagazine.com

Conditions, launched in 2009, is a magazine focusing on the conditions of architecture and urbanism in Scandinavia. The editors seek to present new perspectives for conceiving and analyzing architectural designs, works and theory through regular calls for submissions. 'It is organised in a fluctuating network of agents reflecting the present globalised state of a dynamic society, economics, politics and culture which are the motivators of architecture. Through a play of thoughts in an open-ended forum, predefined 'facts' will be unsecured and constantly reinvented. The forum will gather the architect, client, politician and the public, a communion of ideas creating conditions for evolution.' The magazine is published four times a year.

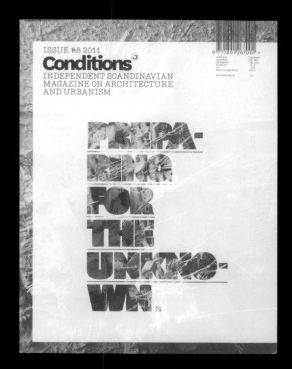

Conditions 8: Preparing for the Unknown, June 2011
200 × 270 mm; 100 pages; 2,000 copies

CORNELL
JOURNAL OF ARCHITECTURE

Ithaca, New York, USA
cornelljournalofarchitecture.
cornell.edu

The *Cornell Journal of Architecture* is a critical journal of architecture and urbanism produced by editors in the Department of Architecture at the College of Architecture, Art and Planning, Cornell University. Established in 1981, the journal was relaunched in 2011 after a decade's absence as an annual publication with editor-in-chief Caroline O'Donnell. It forms a locus for critical discussions emanating from the study of architecture at Cornell. In addition to an open call, student editors solicit texts and drawings from a range of disciplines and locations both inside and outside Cornell University, centred around a specific theme.

Cornell Journal of Architecture 8: RE, January 2011
90 × 155 mm; 194 pages; 1,500 copies

CRITICAT

Paris, France
www.criticat.fr

Launched by Pierre Chabard, Valéry Didelon, Martin Etienne, Françoise Fromonot and Bernard Marey in 2008 as a space for reflection on architecture independent from institutions, *criticat* is a critical review of architecture. The editors believe that since architecture enjoys a privileged position at the heart of politics, society and economics, describing and examining architecture and its issues is a way to critique the world that builds it. To remain independent, *criticat* was formed as an association and relies on support from its readership. *criticat* is sold by mail order from its website.

province

rasoir

architecture

livres

situations

boîte noire

démystifiées

kWh

criticat

cinématographique

olympiques

souvenirs

caviar

numéro 7 / mars 2011

criticat 7, March 2011; 160 × 235 mm; 136 pages; 1,300 copies

DÉRIVE

Vienna, Austria
www.derive.at

dérive is an international interdisciplinary journal focusing
on urbanism that has been published quarterly in Vienna since
2000 by an independent group
of artists, researchers and writers. The magazine juxtaposes
sociology and architecture,
architecture and art, art and
politics, politics and geography,
geography and urban planning,
planning and philosophy,
philosophy and economics.
Most issues focus on a specific
theme explored by experts from
a number of perspectives and
feature urban projects, town
portraits, interviews, articles on
the history of urban life, critical
reviews and unique artwork. Articles are written in German and/
or English, with over 400 contributors – from young scientists
to well established, internation-
ally-acclaimed authors – publishing more than 1,000 articles and
reviews in its first decade.

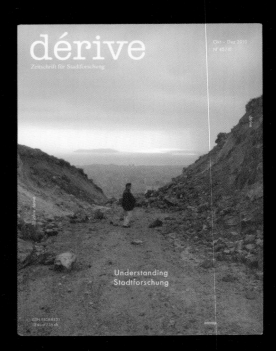

dérive – Magazine for Urban Research 40/41: Understanding
Stadtforschung, October 2010; 210 × 275 mm; 212 pages;
2,500 copies

EIN MAGAZIN ÜBER ORTE

Berlin, Germany
www.orte-magazin.de

Ein Magazin über Orte (A Magazine About Places) is a monothematic magazine which deals with a different location in every issue. The magazine collects works of various authors in the form of photographs, drawings, paintings and texts and is published twice a year. The Home issue tells different stories about the way people are living today and the spaces they inhabit. Published and designed by Elmar Bambach, Julia Marquardt and Birgit Vogel since 2007, other issues include Kitchen, Desk, Crime Scene, Park and Berlin.

Ein Magazin über Orte 6: Home, Winter 2009/10
210 × 270 mm; 84 pages; 1,500 copies

ENGAWA

Barcelona, Spain
www.engawa.es

The *engawa* project launched in January 2010 to provide an open forum to discuss architecture by people located in different cities. The zine takes its name from the transitional space between the interior and exterior of traditional Japanese architecture. The topic of each issue comes from one image chosen by a member of *engawa*. 'After some time our image returns, multiplied, in different articles. It is an experiment based on randomness and the pleasure of sharing thoughts.' In issue four an image of a group of shoes became an essay on a cathedral, the discovery of the addition law in Le Corbusier's Venice Hospital, a story of an imaginary city, a drawing of nude feet and more.

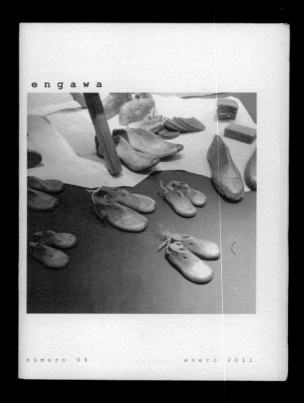

engawa 4, January 2011; 148 × 210 mm; 63 pages; 50 copies and online PDF

EVIL PEOPLE IN MODERNIST HOMES IN POPULAR FILMS

New York City, USA
www.benjamincritton.com

Benjamin Critton launched *Evil People in Modernist Homes in Popular Films* (EPiMHiPF) as an annual zine while studying graphic design at the Yale School of Art. Printed on archival newsprint in red and yellow ink EPiMHiPF offers a serious but lighthearted investigation of the representation of modernist architecture in popular film, reflecting on the convention of associating evil characters and events with modern buildings, and also, more generally, on the relation between cinema and architecture. A series of film stills, quotes and accompanying texts point to examples in *The Damned Don't Cry* (1950), *Diamonds are Forever* (1971), *Blade Runner* (1982), *Body Double* (1984), *Lethal Weapon 2* (1989), *L.A. Confidential* (1997), *The Big Lebowski* (1998) and *Twilight* (2008).

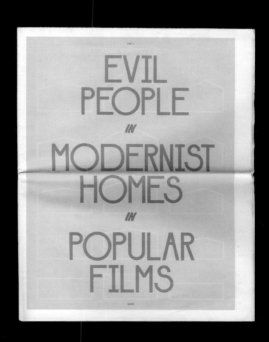

Evil People in Modernist Homes in Popular Films 1,
Summer 2010; 292 × 381 mm; 24 pages; 1,000 copies

FACE B

Paris, France
www.faceb.fr

face b: architecture from the other side is a cultural and architectural journal based in Paris. Launched in 2008 by Sébastien Martinez Barat, Aurélien Gillier and Benjamin Lafore, each issue presents interviews and essays by renowned and emerging critics, curators, architects and artists. '*Back to Basics* defines itself as a break, a moment of wholesome and opportune autarky when architecture withdraws into itself. This issue draws, depicts and forms through the work of architects, a fragile and cold fellowship that can be dissolved at any time. *Back to Basics* does not impoverish history, instead it capitalises vacant referential territories. This issue embodies in its editorial statement, in the curated contributors and in its form what can be called a critical project.'

face b_architecture from the other side

Issue 3_back to basics_
feat. cedric libert, sou fujimoto,
florian idenburg, thomas raynaud, paul mouchet,
office KGDVS, jean-christophe quinton

face b: architecture from the other side 3: Back to Basics
November 2010; 130 × 180 mm; 159 pages; 600 copies

FOREIGN ARCHITECTS SWITZERLAND

Zurich, Switzerland
www.faszine.blogspot.com

Foreign Architects Switzerland (FAS) is a zine dedicated to filling the gaps of theoretical and political dialogue in the Swiss architectural community. *FAS* is meant as a platform for ideas, projects and people that remain illegitimate to the 'brain-dead, incestuous architectural media' of Switzerland. The anonymous editors organise competitions and calls for ideas published in the zine. The first issue set out the *FAS* manifesto, launched the WTF Award and, in reaction to the Swiss minaret ban, called for an open competition for a mosque in Zurich to prove that architects can, and should, be political. *FAS* is posted as a hard copy to 200 architecture offices, institutions and newspapers in and out of Switzerland. The number of publications is restricted; people requesting to be added to the mailing list replace an existing address.

Foreign Architects Switzerland 1, February 2010
210 × 297 mm; 4 pages; 200 copies

FRIENDLY FIRE

Porto, Portugal
www.friendlyfire.info

The first issue of *Friendly Fire* is the result of seven months of conversation about the state of architecture between an independent architecture collective comprising Alexandra Areia, Ivo Poças Martins, Matilde Seabra, Pedro Baía and Pedro Barata Castro. The zine was designed entirely on AutoCad and sets the tone for what is expected to be **a regular editorial project producing 'subversive and humorous narratives and practices' to share with a limited number of readers in Portuguese. Sent selectively by post and sold during a launch event, the zine aims to address the architectural culture and its effects on everyday life in an alternative and informal perspective. *Friendly Fire* operates from a corner shop in the Bouça Housing Complex designed by Álvaro Siza – Porto's first Pritzker Prize laureate.**

Friendly Fire 1: das ist friendly fire, April 2011
145 × 210 mm; 42 pages; 150 copies

MIMI ZEIGER

ON CONTENT, FANDOM AND HOW JAMES DEAN, JARVIS COCKER AND JAMES MURPHY CHANGED ARCHITECTURAL PUBLISHING

In 1998 *Metropolis* magazine ran a short piece on a small, underground trend rising within the world of architecture. 'Architects and planners are no hidden community – they have trade organisations, conferences, and glossy coffee-table journals. But the creators of architecture zines have a different audience in mind', wrote Andrea Mood, explaining that '[T]hey want to turn regular civilians – even those who may never have thought about their surroundings – into architecture fans.'[1] Mood's article was not much more than a few paragraphs long, but in a couple of sentences she captured the essence of what separates a zine from any other type of publication: fandom.

It's impossible to make a zine without being a fan of some kind – a fan of architecture, tiki kitsch, punk rock or Asian pop-culture. The format is governed not by editorial board adjudication or peer review, but by heart-on-your-sleeve enthusiasm for the subject matter lovingly assembled, reproduced and stapled together. Fandom even begins with the history of the publication type. The word 'zine' is derived from 1930s science fiction 'fanzines'. In contrapposto to professional magazines, these amateur publications were written by sci-fi fans and traded by mail within the community.

Zine culture grew, exploding in the late 1980s and early 1990s, as twin forces of Kinko's copy shops and desktop publishing programs made production cheap and accessible. Subject matter included wide swaths of pop culture, but often leaning towards personal, singular themes. Self-produced with small print runs, zine circulation was typically limited to a few dozen, a few hundred or a couple of thousand copies, but the content was always irrepressible. With names like *Bitch*, *Temp Slave* and the *Baffler*, there is a contradictory impulse at work – a non-mainstream embrace of outsider status combined with a desire to connect with a like-minded audience.

Unlike popular magazines, zine production merges the content consumer with the content producer and undermines hierarchies. Of 1980s and 1990s zine culture Steven Duncombe, in his book, *Notes from the Underground, Zines and Politics of Alternative Culture*,[2] writes 'In an era marked by the rapid centralisation of corporate media, zines are independent and localised, coming out of cities, suburbs and small towns across the USA, assembled on kitchen tables. They celebrate the everyperson in a world of celebrity, losers in a society that rewards the best and the brightest.... Zinesters privilege the ethic of DIY, do-it-yourself: make your own culture and stop consuming that which is made for you.'

Historically, architecture as a theme was rare among 90s-era zines, which tended to focus on the rough edges of alternative culture: punk rock (*Maximum Rock and Roll*), identity politics (*Bikini Kill*, *Chickfactor*, *Fanorama*, *Giant Robot*), and kitsch (*Beer Frame* and *Thrift Score*). In her write-up on architecture zines, Mood listed *Monorail*, a one-off, 23-page zine dedicated solely to the titular subject matter. Zinester Steve Mandich first published *Monorail* in October 1996, with a follow-up printing in July 1998.[3] While the topic today may seem to align with contemporary architecture's preoccupations with urban infrastructure, at the time it existed at the edge of architectural interest. Mandich is better known as the personality behind *Heinous*, a beloved publication with an obsession with anything to do with daredevil Evel Knievel including the treatise: 'Field Guide to Evel Knievel's Injuries'. His publishing prowess was one-part fandom and one-part production, or rather taking advantage of the tedium of a day job. 'I work in production for a certain national chain of photocopy stores that rhymes with "Stinkos",' he said in a 1996 interview with Chip Rowe, author of the *Book of Zines: Reading from the Fringe*.[4]

Mandich's argument for covering monorails boiled down simply to the fact that they are cool. The zine gave him the excuse to explore the history of Seattle Alweg Monorail, which debuted at the 1962 World's Fair: The Century 21 Exposition. It's tempting to discount *Monorail* as ephemeral and driven by personal research. However, it's precisely this subjectivity that gives Mandich a desire to reach a larger, like-minded public, as seen in his answer to a question I asked him about the origin of the publication: 'It began as a proposed article about Seattle's monorail, a one-mile relic from the 1962 World's Fair, for Dan Howland's excellent *Journal of Ride Theory*. Yet the more I researched the subject, the bigger the piece grew, until it made sense to turn it into a zine of its own.' Mandich's response reveals the interconnectedness of zine culture and the trading of favours and enthusiasms as promoted by DIY (Do-It-Yourself) ethos. He continued, 'Since [*Monorail*'s] publication, Seattle residents (myself included, as I moved back here in '98) voted to build a citywide monorail system. Sadly, due to financing problems, the project was scrapped.'[5]

Architecture zines, like the little magazines of the 60s and 70s, thrive on pop culture – absorbing and disseminating influences.[6] Urban forms are sucked into zine culture just as readily as jumpsuited daredevils, with just as much passion for the subject. For instance, the zine *GO* focuses its efforts on Sheffield, a bombed-out, run-down former steel town filled with towers of housing flats. (It is also the birthplace of Pulp and its frontman Jarvis Cocker, a fact the *GO* editors gleefully promote.) '*GO* is a fanzine about Sheffield. The best city in the world', write zine creators Tom Keeley and Tom James. Issue 7, entitled 'Sheffield is beautiful', is a love letter written with little irony. The introduction clarifies in no uncertain terms an indulgence in the urban realm and a devotion to wooing a wide audience: '[W]e're not just talking about post-industrial beauty. Not just trying to convince you that Forgemasters is prettier than Paris. Sheffield has old-people-pleasing beauty too.'[7]

Still, there's an inherent conflict within zine culture and with fandom in general: are these public or private enthusiasms? In Keeley, Jones, and Mandich's cases the private provokes public outreach, but with other small publications, the trajectory isn't as clear. The prose used to express undying passion for a subject is often written so hastily that it proves a barrier to entry and a mark of street cred. In the pages of *Subculture: the Meaning of Style*, Dick Hebdige captures the insistent language of zines not in the actual words, but in the form of the text:

'The language in which the various manifestoes were framed was determinedly "working class" (i.e. it was liberally peppered with swear words) and typing errors and grammatical mistakes, misspellings and jumbled pagination were left uncorrected in the final proof. ... The overwhelming impression was one of urgency and immediacy, of a paper produced in indecent haste, of memos from the front line.'[8]

Or, as Rowe – the crotchety zinester and former editor of the zine sourcebook, *Fact Sheet Five* – bluntly puts it, 'Most zines suck'.[9]

Zines, in this indecent relationship to pop culture, form a discursive space between poles – between mainstream and what used to be called 'alternative' culture, between professional and amateur, between the academy and the everyday. For architecture, this is useful space for acting out enthusiasms – activist, political or personal – not sanctioned by the traditional canon.

It is important to understand zines within their historical context – a time stratified by production technologies and broadcasting reach. In the years since, network culture and social media: blogs, Twitter, Facebook, have irrevocably blurred disciplinary distinctions. But in 1992, when architect Michelle Fornabai published the fanzine *Death Drive* as part of her Master of Architecture thesis project at Princeton University, she saw the format as a means to connect with a network of James Dean fans.

Death Drive is about the stretch of road along California State Highway 46 just east of

Cholame, California where James Dean died when his silver Porsche Spyder crashed into an oncoming vehicle. Fornabai was interested in the kind of fan culture developing at the site and proposed in her publication a kind of 'cult architecture' to accommodate related activities. Although her thesis programme included an exhibition space, as well as a drag strip (à la *Rebel Without a Cause*), crash simulators and a bar, her zine uses narrative first person diary entries to describe the site and the architecture. As a result, she implicates herself in the cultish rituals of James Dean fandom. In some notes she made at the time about *Death Drive*, she writes:

> '"Cult" remains linked to "pop culture" – working from a ground within the very boundaries seemingly transgressed. Cult architecture avoids a search for "generic popular taste" in terms delineated by pop art, or a complete unproblematic embrace of popular culture (Venturi), which only reinforces the status quo. "Cult" signals a feared or ominous difference, organised minority beliefs that threaten the status quo, taboo intellectual territory outside of mainstream values... It constitutes a refusal to create new types to be consumed, working instead with cultural debris, the abject trash of popular culture in a recycling, a series of transformations and surreal manifestations.'[10]

According to Fornabai, she only published 50 to 150 copies of her 54-page, colour-xeroxed booklet, but a small print-run didn't discourage her impulse to use it to broaden to the reach of architecture, as she explains in the same notes. 'Cult architecture seeks to critically engage a common ground – popular culture – to bring architectural discourse beyond the walls of the university and the profession.'

Going 'beyond the walls' of academia is a self-reflexive imperative inherent in architectural zinedom and is perhaps what differentiates it as a publishing practice from your average punk rock zine. A music fan isn't necessarily interested in interdisciplinary exchange. To wit, when I began my zine, *loud paper*, in 1997 as my own Master of Architecture thesis at SCI-Arc in Los Angeles, I started with a broadminded call for submissions: 'As the world of architectural publishing is polarised into the camps of professional pragmatism and academic theory, *loud paper* is staunchly neither. *Loud paper* is open to all students, architects, educators, girls about town, dear Johns and critics as a place for writing loud about architecture and culture.'[11]

I saw the format and the content of the zine as a way to not only represent my own personal voice and architectural fandom, but as an opportunity to connect with other architects of my generation who were writing about architecture but unable to find publishing venues. To understand this position, we have to recall that the mid-1990s represent a lull in alternative architectural publishing in the United States. Websites were only just beginning to represent independent publishing platforms and journals such as *Any*, *October* and *Assemblage* were their domain and outgrowth of existing academic structures and the critical theory establishment. In the years after *loud paper* launched, a number of younger, nimble architecture publications came into existence, including, *Praxis*, *30/60/90*, and the online forum Archinect.

Just as zines merge consumers and producers, emerging writers, artists, architects and designers were not only *loud paper*'s audience, but also its chief contributors. The publication carries the subtitle 'dedicated to increasing the volume of architectural discourse', the pun an intentional stance against homogeneity within architectural discourse. The intent was to encourage louder and more discussions. By partnering with contributors from other fields, *loud paper* was able to cover art, music and pop culture as well as design and continually question the process of disseminating architecture outside of its normally confined venues. These collaborations go beyond the zine itself to the formation of a network of people whose fandom extends to leveraging self-publishing as a legitimate site of architectural production.

A publication such as *Losing (our) Edge: Leagues & Legions metatext x.1*, edited by Fred Scharmen of the blog sevensixfive.com, represents the future of zines in a digital world. Produced and distributed using the print-on-demand service Lulu, *Losing (our) Edge* is an experiment in aggregation and the relationships between print and web. Scharmen compiled blog posts, copying and pasting essays and comments from fellow bloggers including Dan Hill, Enrique Ramirez, Rob Holmes, and Adam Greenfield. The entries range in time from fall 2009 to winter 2010 and each approaches the subject of disciplinary boundaries within architecture and design from a different angle. Any comments and links within and between pieces are cross-indexed or 'linked' across the publication with page numbers replacing URLs.

Zine-like, the publication alights on the edge of fandom. Ramirez's post 'Architecture Against the System (1): Electric Lightning' from his blog aggregat456.com begins with a discussion of the Lightning supersonic fighter, an aircraft written about by Reyner Banham in a 1960 issue of *The Architectural Review*. Ramirez makes sure to call Banham out as an 'aviation enthusiast'.[12] However it's the title of the pamphlet that reveals Scharmen as a music fan. *Losing (our) Edge* is cribbed from the LCD Soundsystem's song 'Losing My Edge'. He includes James Murphy's song lyrics – an embittered paean about the anxieties of cool – giving them the same weight as any of the essays. Scharmen's small publication skirts the demands and constraints of dominant architectural taste and also is testament to collective platforms and discursive channels in a digital age.

While the mechanisms of zine publishing – mail-order distribution and photocopy reproduction – have been replaced by downloadable PDFs, e-books and print-on-demand services, the DIY ethos remains a point of connectivity. The relationships built in print are strengthened and expanded with social media tools. And from blogs, Twitter and Facebook dialogues come new publications that are actively derived from a thriving discourse.

Focusing on zine content reveals a lesson in how to actively use fandom to rework and expand the limits of architectural production. For example, *Junk Jet* publishers Asli Serbest and Mona Mahall routinely choose outré themes for their 'lo-fi paper publication'.[13] The titles of their four issues to date tell it all: noise-and-failure!, speculative-architecture!, flux-us! flux-you!, and statistics-of-mystics! Each exclamation point conveys a straight shot of enthusiasm for the subject, but it is also a deliberate yelp: a way to break through the staid conversational tones found in contemporary publishing.

Still, there's a tendency to focus on format when discussing independent publications. The relationship between digital media and the written word continually revises itself as technologies change and develop. If we look only at a zine as a representation of format, we're prone to a nostalgic embrace of print. As the old format – staple and folded pamphlets – is replaced by internet memes and Tumblr feeds as a means to *indulge* in the personal, subcultural and pop, zines still revel in the subjective. Publishers choose print and mutant methods that bridge between paper and digital[14] precisely because they are boosters of the medium and the freedom it represents, regardless of topic. Or, as Giancarlo Valle, Isaiah King and Ryan Neiheiser write: 'Against the haze of digital distraction, we crave an object to hold our attention – something to touch, to fold, to tuck in our back pocket, to discard.'[15] As editors of the newcomer zine *another pamphlet*, they feel the need to defend their self-described anachronistic choice of print and express their zine fandom. In an ouroboros relationship between content and format, subject and object, we now see that what

67

was once a delivery device – a small folio containing individualised and obscure passions – is now
the thing to be adored.

NOTES

1. Andrea Mood, 'The
   Zine-ing of Architecture,'
   Metropolis, May 1998.
2. Steven Duncombe,
   *Notes from the Underground,
   Zines and Politics of Alternative Culture*, Verso Books,
   1997, p 2
3. Steve Mandich, *Monorail*,
   Issue Number One,
   October 1996 and July 1998.
4. http://www.zinebook.
   com/interv/heinous.html
5. email interview: Mimi
   Zeiger and Steve Mandich.
   November 2008.
6. As discussed in the
   book and exhibition *Clip/
   Stamp/Fold*, http://www.
   clipstampfold.com. Most
   notably seen in Archigram's
   fourth issue of their
   eponymous magazine,
   Amazing Archigram / Zoom,
   which not only featured
   a sci-fi theme, but also
   the now iconic comic book
   style cover designed by
   Warren Chalk.
7. Tom Jones and Tom Keeley,
   GO, issue 7, 'Sheffield is
   Beautiful', Summer 2005.
8. Dick Hebdige, *Subcul-
   ture: the Meaning of Style*,
   Routledge, 1987, New York.
   p 111.
9. Chip Rowe, 'Whatcha
   Mean What's a Zine?', *The
   Book of Zines, Readings from
   the Fringe*, 1997.
10. Michelle Fornabai, notes
    from the author, 1993-94.
11. Mimi Zeiger, *loud paper*,
    volume 1, issue 1, 1997.
12. Ramirez, Enrique, 'Archi-
    tecture Against the System
    (1): Electric Lighting',
    aggregat456.com, January
    24, 2010.
13. http://junkjet.net/
14. Mimi Zeiger, 'Blue Lob-
    sters', *Junk Jet* no 3 flux-us!
    flux-you!, January 2010,
    p 112. http://books.google.
    de/books?id=2Owf4MiZK
    HIC&pg=PA5&source=
    gbs_selected_pages&cad=
    3#v=onepage&q&f=false
15. anotherpamphlet.com/
    pamphlet.html

GENERALIST

Frankfurt am Main, Germany
www.generalist.in

Launched in 2008 to discuss and popularise current debates as well as practical and theoretical trends in architecture, urban design and other related professions, *GENERALIST* seeks to provide broad, multidisciplinary editorial content. The magazine combines different professional perspectives on specific subjects that annotate current tendencies and developments. Published in English and German text, editors Björn Hekmati, Frank Metzger, Insa Reichenau and Adeline Seidel require all contributions, whether analysis, interpretation or a particular position, to be structured as open discussions. Responding to the current economic climate, the fourth issue of *GENERALIST* offers different responses to 'saving' in architecture, design and the urban realm.

GENERALIST 4: Saving / Sparen, February 2011
210 × 297 mm; 70 pages; 1,000 copies

HORIZONTE

Weimar, Germany
m18.uni-weimar.de/horizonte

Students at the Bauhaus-Universität Weimar launched their own architecture journal in 2010 loosely based on weekly lectures at the student initiative *Horizonte*. With interviews, essays, photography and projects, each issue addresses one singular subject. The journal's focus is on questions that pertain to the relationship between architecture and society and provides a platform for discussing current architectural topics from a student's perspective, alongside publishing works of established professionals, theorists and practitioners. Published twice a year, *Horizonte – Journal for Architectural Discourse* is an interdisciplinary and collaborative effort between the faculties of architecture, design and media studies and is set up as an independent student organisation.

Horizonte – Journal for Architectural Discourse 3: Re-definition,
April 2011; 150 × 230 mm; 144 pages; 700 copies

JUNK JET

Stuttgart, Germany
www.junkjet.net

Junk Jet is conceived as a 'zine-jet', a collaborative format set up to discuss speculative works on topics of architecture, media, aesthetics and electronics. It is an irregular publication (including irrational special gifts) on a non-commercial scale edited by Asli Serbest and Mona Mahall and published by their own igmade.edition. *Junk Jet* is interested in 'counter works (and counter counter works) of counter aesthetics, tunnelling practices that show lack of any irony or fiction. It is about wild forms and found objects, about weird theories and (small) narratives, anti-fashions and non-styles, about exploring do-it-yourself works, accidental outcomes, deviant and normal aesthetic forms that result from jammed common practices, misused media, and subverted customary tools.'

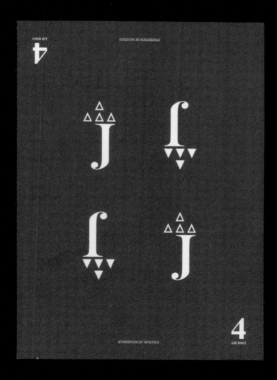

Junk Jet 4: Statistics-of-Mystics!, October 2010
190 × 270 mm; 88 pages; 888 copies

KERB

Melbourne, Australia
www.kerb19.com

Kerb is a landscape architecture journal produced by students from RMIT University. The journal is an annual publication edited each year by a new team of students who curate a collection of projects and articles relevant to topical themes. A total restructure in 2010 provided a new level of focus and identity for the journal. *Kerb* 19 is the first issue to be produced under this new model and explores how the development of bio-technological possibilities will shape the way we create landscapes where the city environment could transform into a dynamic, interactive organism of limitless potential.

Kerb 19: Paradigms of Nature: Post Natural Futures
September 2011; 210 × 297 mm; 130 pages; 2,000 copies

ance
cialez.fr

d twice a year by the
éciale d'Architecture
Le Journal Spéciale'Z
architecture, art and
n, bringing together
c research, interviews,
tary, narrative and

projects. The journal favo
emerging voices and orig
critical investigations. It i
structured around themat
questions announced in n
ly, open calls for submissi
Recent themes include D
tion, Resistance, Number
Revisiting the Vernacular

le Journal
Spéciale'Z
n°02

les Thèmes
Disorder
Horizon(tal)
Decolonization & Architecture
Narration

ÉCOLE
SPÉCIALE
D'ARCHITECTURE

City, USA
corp.com

…rvations on Architecture *…ontemporary City* is …for new architectural …nd criticism. A com- …of essays, conversa- …short observations …nporary buildings and …*og* eschews the visual

in favour of determined into the critical and cult implications of the disci Recent topics include: th necessity of the metacri in architecture; burgeon urbanism in Dubai; lying images; and unanswerab questions posed by signa buildings. *Log* is publish three times a year.

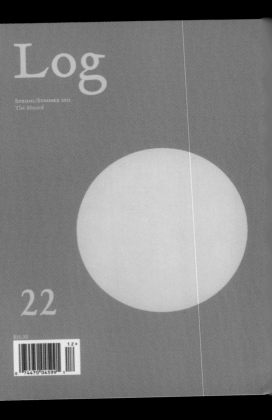

Log

Spring/Summer 2011
The Absurd

22

$15.00

12>

0 74470 04599 1

MAP

Copenhagen, Denmark
www.map.davidgarciastudio.com

Published twice a year by David Garcia Studio, *MAP (Manual of Architectural Possibilities)* presents itself as a folded A1 poster where information is immediate, dense and objective on one side, and architectural and subjective on the other. *MAP* is 'a guide to potential actions in the built environment, a folded encyclopedia of the possible, a topography of ideas, or a poster on the wall'. Issue 4 deals with the spatial implications of flooding with projects in the Netherlands, Italy, the USA and the Maldives.

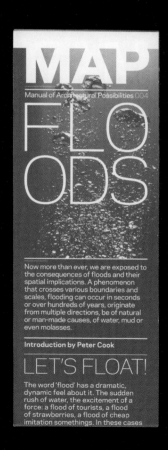

MAP 4: Floods, September 2011; 105 × 297 mm folded;
841 x 594 mm unfolded; 2,000 copies

MARK

Amsterdam, Netherlands;
www.mark-magazine.com

Mark was launched in 2005 with three guiding principles: the first is a radically international perspective; the second is viewing the magazine as a visual medium; the third is the attempt to escape jargon and academicism. The magazine sets out to seduce and enchant, and address the visual intelligence of today's reader. With a strong focus on image and aesthetics, the bi-monthly magazine is more closely aligned to the style press than traditional architectural publishing and in this way presents itself as alternative.

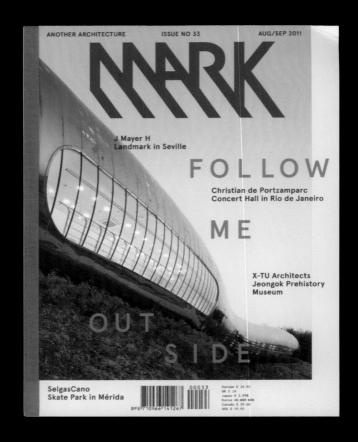

Mark 33, August/September 2011; 230 × 297 mm; 224 pages; 19,000 copies

MAS CONTEXT

Chicago, USA
www.mascontext.com

MAS Context is a quarterly journal launched by MAS Studio in 2009 to address issues affecting the urban context. It aims to provide a comprehensive view of a topic by the active participation of people from different fields and different perspectives; to instigate the debate. Published four times per year, every issue is centred on a single topic. With a global approach and reach, it is a platform of discussion and collaboration where relevant proposals, ideas and experiences are shared to help advance the design field. Contributions take the form of essays, photographs, diagrams, interviews and case studies. The journal is currently available online, as a free downloadable PDF, and as a print-on-demand publication.

MAS Context 10: Conflict, Summer 2011; 152 × 228 mm; 140 pages; print-on-demand and online PDF

MATZINE

Dublin, Ireland;
London / Dundee, UK
matzine.wordpress.com

matzine is a collaborative publication which dwells on the peripheries of architecture, and through its inquiries traverses art, illustration, historical reflections, experimental writing and more. Launched in 2009, *matzine* originated from the desire of a group of MArch students at the Dundee School of Architecture to quickly disseminate initial research ideas and to explore cheap, independent publication. It has expanded to include contributions from many disciplines and geographies, and with each issue a new editor brings original thematic focus. Contributions have included short essays, drawings, photographs and video. *matzine* is published online as a free digital edition and a print-ready PDF which anyone may print and distribute.

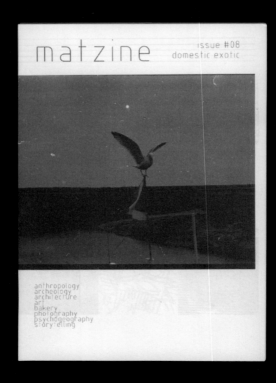

matzine 8: Domestic Exotic, April 2011; 148 × 210 mm; 40 pages; 200 copies and online PDF

MAXIMUM MAXIM MMX

New York City, USA
www.loudpaper.typepad.com

Maximum Maxim MMX is a fanzine from Mimi Zeiger, editor of the ongoing New York-based zine project *loud paper*, and is maximised with maxims germane to architecture and publishing. According to Zeiger, the popularity of the aphorism, a short, memorable, often pithy statement, goes hand in hand with the invention of printing. Although print remains precarious in a digital age, the aphoristic statement lives on. According to Oscar Wilde 'In the old days books were written by men of letters and read by the public. Now books are written by the public and read by nobody.' *Maximum Maxim MMX* was first presented at Storefront for Art and Architecture's Book Launch Cabaret in 2010.

Maximum Maxim MMX, October 2010; 140 × 215 mm; 68 pages; 100 copies

MEGAWORDS

New York City, USA
www.megawordsmagazine.com

The mission of *Megawords* magazine is 'to document our surroundings and experience, to have a voice free from the noise of commercialisation and competing novelties, and to create an open and active dialogue between *Megawords* and the community'. As well as self-publishing the magazine since 2005, founders Anthony Smyrski and Dan Murphy exhibit in galleries and museums across the United States, and organise events and performances under the banner *Megawords*.

Megawords 15, April 2010; 265 × 320 mm; 32 pages; 3,000 copies

PEDRO GADANHO

ON EXPERIMENTAL ARCHITECTURAL WRITING AND ITS MEDIA

'Dear reader, before you start to read this, you should be aware that this is not your typical piece of criticism. Architectural criticism is being nailed at its crossroads, and the critic feels embarrassed by such an instance. She can only mirror this moment of truth.

The critic sits in her office busy with her private quests and investigations. The critic has been trying to lose the label of being a critic. She has been refusing the role. She is aware of the uneasy stance of the profession these days. She prefers to see herself as a writer. She likes to write.

A far from odd request suddenly lands on her laptop. It comes from afar, through a foreign intermediary. A magazine on the other side of the world requires a review of four recent buildings. There is a theme connecting the disparate objects: safety and emergency programmes.

The building that lies closest to the critic is not far: 461 km. Another one lies a mere 2,744 km away. The farthest is 3,713 km. Google maps says it would take 1 day and 15 hours to get there. The critic sits back and enjoys the prospect of a quick pan-European trip. She likes to travel.

Romantically, she clings for a moment to an old-fashioned idea. Once upon a time, the critic had to experience the architecture to talk about it. She imagines travelling by car for three days, 21 hours and 10 minutes to visit these buildings. She could visit friends in Paris on her way back.

'The speed and economics of the contemporary world have made me an analyst of visual culture', she muses to herself. She looks at about 20-30 different buildings everyday. In this flow, she dedicates a few seconds to each work. One image is enough to dismiss a building.

She finds herself amused by turning this exercise in visual information accumulation into a different mode of analysis. She remembers colleagues who dedicated painful amounts of time to comparing plans and sections to photographic images of beloved buildings. She envied their patience.

She looks at the images of one of the buildings sent to her in a zip file. It's a fire station in Bergen. It dates from 2007 and it already looks dated. Dating an object, like one does in archaeology, is a curious process. It says a lot. It says time is merciless.

She reflects that the shape and materiality of this building could have arisen anywhere between 1987 and... 2007. To say the least. If you were looking back on it 200 years ahead, this building would be simply indistinguishable. She sighs.

What would future architecture archaeologists dig out of this object? The last remains of an enduring Nordic modernism, mixed with a properly sustainable, vaguely postmodern design sensibility. Alvar Aalto turned into an honest, slightly boring middlebrow production.

In distress, the critic turns to the architect's description of his own building. She looks for redemption. He comes back with 'magnificent views', 'the negative appearance of the traffic' and 'the building as part of a future settlement'. She feels she is suffocating in obviousness.

Maybe she is being unfair. Unconsciously, maybe the building speaks of a candid willingness to provide a last glimpse of architectural social welfare in a burning Europe. On the other hand, the critic realises she probably longs for a fire station straight out of a Ray Bradbury novel.

The critic is reminded of other fire stations. She visited Vitra's many years ago. Zaha Hadid used to be a surprising architect – until her formal recipe killed her relevance. One could well dwell on the ironies of a fire station made out of languid concrete flames and acute blazing spaces.

She remembers delightful fire station towers that would mesh up different bits of city. To simulate emergency action, they would assemble disparate parts of buildings in an absurd functionalist fashion. True Colin Rowe collectibles. She takes a mental note for further research.

Incidentally, the critic recalls why her profession was made obsolete by the beginning of the twenty-first century. Do we really need motives and arguments? As former New York Times critic Paul Goldberger stated, 'nobody tears down a building if the architecture critic doesn't like it'.

The critic then turned her attention onto the next building.'1

5

The piece of writing transcribed above was the meta-critical answer to a very typical commission by a respectable, mainstream architectural magazine of international scope. The editors, though, have very diplomatically rejected the proposal. They were honestly concerned about the way in which their architectural readership would receive the text.

6

Independent magazines and publications are desperately needed in any cultural field. One of the reasons for this permanent urgency lies in the fact that, particularly in the midst of an increasingly market-oriented, mainstream production, their enthusiastic and entrepreneurial editors are willing to build their imagined readership out of a respect for the audience's capability to welcome alternative ways of thinking (and writing).

7

Independent, with its dangerous closeness to potentially subversive notions such as *non-dependent, self-ruling* and *autonomous*, sometimes represents the very opposite of *academic*. Namely, independent thought resides in the very antipodes of the necessity of academia to constantly delimit and affirm its borders and *status quo*. Personal *ways of thinking* (and writing) defy the need to establish social and technical normatives in which an impending mediocracy is better able to thrive.

8

Nowadays, for instance, applying for a conference with a paper proposal, is only fun as long as you train your ability to write in *a certain way*, using *a certain jargon*, employing *the right references*. Once you've dominated that particular apparatus, however, you may feel anxious about the formality – and emptiness – of such an exercise. The same may apply to those self-important magazines that, at any given time, are entitled by the establishment to dictate what the architectural world should be thinking about. They predictably tend to fall prisoners to the builders of convention.

9

I
mean,
perhaps
one
should
write
with
invisible
ink.

10

As against the 'crisis of criticism', are we facing a *fictional turn* in the writing of architecture? Beatriz, smart as she always has been, warned us about six years ago that 'architecture should learn from fiction'. She cleverly advanced that 'fiction is irreverent and irrelevant'. And she added that fiction's power precisely 'comes from this'.[2] However, fiction as a literary machine is more than irreverent, and far from irrelevant. It offers a prospect of *critical practice*: by way of the ability to write the apparently *unwritable*; in the accuracy of text over fact as a *critical device*; with its demand for an *open meaning and interpretation*; through its goal of reaching for the *reader('s active role)*. Will spell this out some other day.

11

Perhaps architectural writing doesn't really have to be about *criticism*. Nor, for that matter, even about the *truth* (as that member of the audience in Montreal sharply hinted at[3]). Maybe I just want my writing to be *out there as another practice*. Like Irit Rogoff, I want it to be 'a "writing with" an artist's work, rather than about it'. As she reasons, this will create a 'dehierarchisation' in the delicate issue of who has today 'the final word in determining the meaning of a work'.[4] Definitely, it points in the direction of a clearly *autonomous production*. And then this *writing* can be a fiction, a theoretical exploit, an essayistic experience, a blog post or an automated script. As long as it's *good writing*, as long as the relevance of its contents upholds the attention of the audience, it will do. (Not an easy task, though.)

89

In her essay 'What is a Theorist?', Rogoff addresses issues of so-called *knowledge production*. If the current experimental modes of writing are not purely engaged in *entertainment*, then they must surely constitute alternative ways to *question* and *produce* knowledge. Conversely, to some people's aversion, the sites of knowledge are indeed shifting away from their traditional contexts and settings. Rogoff speaks of *'practice-driven theory'* and tells us of 'theoretical surges whose drive and impetus might have come from the experience of art and other practices, with their permissions to start from elsewhere, to not rehearse great swaths of prior knowledge, to invent viewing positions and contextual fictions'. *Different positions*, *utterly unexpected* *formats and media*, she's uttering, may suddenly be a valid starting point for the invention of the previously unthinkable.

13

Translator Richard Howard writing on Roland Barthes reminds us of the latter's fierce determination to assert 'the pleasure we must take in our reading as against the indifference of (mere) knowledge'. Barthes himself evoked the *writerly bliss* as that which 'unsettles the reader's historical, cultural, psychological assumptions', a specific event that 'brings a crisis to his relation with language.'[5] Meanwhile, it sounds as though architecture has only recently come to be seen as a form of knowledge, a language that is related to something more than just erecting buildings. Now that its erogenous zones have been reallocated, maybe the bliss of writing (and reading) on architectural matters can be about something else. It may now be about merrily upturning our liaison to architecture's very foundations, instead of further tying us down to its fundamentalisms, its recurring institutional incarcerations, and its plain unfortunate downturns.

As the author of another dead blog, Steve Parnell, put it in one of his last posts at the *The Sesquipedalist*: 'Criticism gets a bad press because it's perceived as being about finding problems with things, or searching for the poor. But that's just the obvious and easy side of criticism. Good criticism is difficult. It needs to be intelligent, witty, insightful, knowledgeable, authoritative, accessible, and a host of other adjectives that make it as much a productive art as the thing that it's criticising. In addition, being a critic is far from glamorous. The architectural press run countless awards and competitions to "nurture architectural talent" while ignoring the nurturing of the very stuff that goes into making a great architectural magazine – criticism. Perhaps this is one reason our architectural magazines are so wanting these days. Although it's highly questionable whether better criticism in the architectural press can improve the quality of our built environment, it may at least make better reading.'6

15

As Manfredo Tafuri could have provocatively put it, 'it is a writer's job to look after his sentences. Nothing else.'[7] Similar murdering ideas allowed him to single-handedly discharge the responsibility of criticism to affect the course of architecture practice. And while he nihilistically emptied out the possibilities of architectural writing for generations to come – and created a catastrophic, yet cherished recession in the relationship between architecture and its discourses – he pointed to an unavoidable truth: writing is in itself an autonomous practice and is thus entitled to bite any hand that feeds it. Moreover, this very autonomy is also what gives writing the promising grace of indeed being able to influence the thinking of others. This influence, however, and as Barthes would have put it, is only achievable through *pleasure*. Only when architectural writers recognise and assume this many-sided, complex self-sufficiency – while vehemently resisting the hypnotism of architecture's own autonomy – will they restore the lost splendour of what Tafuri wickedly dismissed as *operative criticism*.

All of the above being stated, one should note that this text was itself experimentally shaped with a key consideration in mind. It surely aspired to respond to the publication curator's challenge to ascertain why it is again critically imperative for creative, fictional and personal narratives to be inventive in regards to architectural discourse and practice. Essentially, though, the piece aimed at awarding as much intellectual pleasure as it possibly could to both its writer and its readers. Thus, its construction had to derive from the autonomous world of writing (and reading), more than that of practising architecture and its discursive (dis)contents. Even so, the geometrical and spatial premises of the text are akin to the self-imposed rules architects employ so as to trigger and sustain their creative process when designing. As the initial fictional story is a rhythmic experience close to the terse format of the aphorism, the remaining text grows from it in an arithmetical progression preset by chapter 14 and the piece's imposed length. Hidden formal strategies to design content and present ideas are, after all, a crucial part of any self-respecting autonomous practice.

NOTES

1. See Pedro Gadanho, '*Salon des Refusés #01*', in Shrapnel Contemporary, 25 May 2011. As visited at http://shrapnel-contemporary.wordpress.com/2011/05/25/salon-des-refuses-01/, September 2011.

2. See Beatriz Colomina, 'Architecture should learn from fiction', in *VOLUME* 1, 2005, Amsterdam.

3. As contributed to the conversation 'On experimental writing,' held at the Canadian Centre for Architecture on 10 February 2011. Recording (Part 3; 28'10) available September 2011 at http://www.cca.qc.ca/system/items/6161/original/Experimental_Writing_2_.mp3?1298067114.

4. See Irit Rogoff in 'What is a Theorist?', in Maria Hlavajova, Jill Winder, and Binna Choi (eds), *On Knowledge Production: a Critical Reader in Contemporary Art*, Utrecht and Frankfurt, BAK & Revolver, 2008

5. See Roland Barthes, *Le Plaisir du Text*, Éditions du Seuil, Paris, 1973

6. See Steve Parnell, 'Forward to 5 Seventy 3', in The Sesquipedalist, 26 May 2010. As visited at http://sesquipedalist.blogspot.com/2010/05/forward-to-5-seventy-3.html, September 2011.

7. The claim, upon a quote from John McGahern, is advanced by Teresa Stoppani in her article 'The Building of Tension – ManfredoTafuri's Legacy: from Operative Criticism to Historical Project, Between Critical Practices and Material Practices in Architecture', from the proceedings of *Reflections on Creativity: Exploring the Role of Theory in Creative Practices*, Duncan of Jordanstone College, 2007, Dundee.

hester, UK
the-modernist-mag.co.uk

Modernist, published quar-
by the Manchester Mod-
Society, was launched in
2011 as 'a quarterly maga-
bout twentieth-century
n'. It combines the DIY

ethos of the society with a
sign influenced by the mode
graphics and typography of
postwar period. Under the
torship of Jack Hale and Ma
reen Ward, the magazine pu
lishes contributions that sh
an affection for the twentie
century built environment
modern, brutalist architect

«a quarterly magazine about
twentieth century design»

Issue No. 2
brilliant

the modernist

Foreword by Phil Griffin
Stirling in Runcorn
Brilliant Light
Light, More Light
An Arndale for Living
Holidays in Utopia
Hard Brilliance
Conran Before Habitat
Stella Maris
William Mitchell
Book Reviews
Diary

£3.75

9772046290004   02

MONO.KULTUR

Berlin, Germany
www.mono-kultur.com

The concept for the independent magazine published by Kai von Rabenau is simple: one issue, one interview. Every issue of *mono.kultur* is dedicated entirely to one artist from across the cultural spectrum and contains one extensive and in-depth interview. Carefully edited and designed, each issue is adapted to and produced in close co-operation with the given interview partner leading to bespoke design solutions. Architects interviewed in *mono. kultur* include MVRDV and David Adjaye.

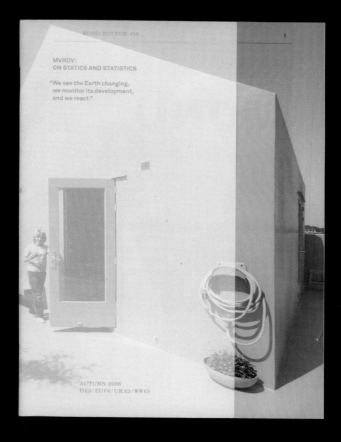

mono.kultur 18: MVRDV: On Statics and Statistics, Autumn 2008
150 × 200 mm; 44 pages; 5,000 copies

MONU

Rotterdam, Netherlands
www.monu-magazine.com

MONU – magazine on urbanism is a bi-annual international forum for artists, writers and designers who are working on topics of urban culture, development and politics. Each issue collects essays, projects and photographs from contributors from all over the world providing a variety of perspectives on a given topic. It was launched in 2004 as a small, stapled together, black-and-white publication. Overseen by editor-in-chief Bernd Upmeyer together with his Rotterdam-based Bureau of Architecture, Research and Design (BOARD) and managing editor Beatriz Ramo, *MONU* now provides a platform for comparative urban analysis, with contributions from Tokyo, Thailand, Detroit, Los Angeles, London and many other cities.

MONU – magazine on urbanism 14: Editing Urbanism, April 2011
200 × 270 mm; 132 pages; 3,000 copies

NO NOW

New York City, USA
www.nonow.net

no now is a publishing venture from Melissa J Frost and Shannon M O'Neill. 'We make and make available carefully constructed publications because we believe in something: architecture, urbanism, history, art, literature, libraries and long walks on the beach.' Frost's handmade zine, *Towards an Architecture of Opposition*, is an exploration of current attempts at architecture as activism and provides '20 pages of architecture criticism at its most punk rock'. 'When a scathing political critique of activist architecture had to be toned down for an institutional magazine, I realised a zine would be a more appropriate format to say what I needed to with complete honesty and freedom. I put it together by hand in the copy shop and sold it at cost just to get it out there to friends and peers in order to start dialogues.'

Towards an Architecture of Opposition 1, October 2010
101mm × 127 mm; 24 pages; 80 copies

OASE

Rotterdam, Netherlands
www.oasejournal.nl

OASE is an independent peer-reviewed journal that brings together academic discourse and the sensibilities of design practice. Three thematic issues are published each year. Originally launched in 1983 by the architectural students at the Delft Faculty, since 2003 *OASE* is published by NAi Publishers reaching a new, international audience. The editors – Tom Avermaete, David de Bruijn, Job Floris, Christoph Grafe, Klaske Havik, Anne Holtrop, Ruben Molendijk, Véronique Patteeuw, Hans Teerds, Gus Tielens, Tom Vandeputte – insist on the discussion of the historical and theoretical aspects of contemporary design issues, bridging the gap between theory and practice. *OASE* 81 offers both theoretical arguments concerning the limits and the domain of criticism, opinions on the role of architecture criticism and identifies potential fields of action while offering tentative explorations of criticism in practice.

OASE 81: Constructing Criticism; July 2010; 170 × 240 mm; 144 pages; 1,500 copies

ONE:TWELVE

Columbus, Ohio, USA
www.ksacommunity.osu.edu/
group/onetwelve

One:Twelve is a self-funded, student-run magazine at Ohio State University. It was launched by Greg Evans and Josh Kuhr to provide a cohesive student voice that connects the disciplines of architecture, landscape architecture and planning at the Knowlton School of Architecture to the campus community and the broader discourse. 'As a student collaborative searching for the voice of the Knowlton School of Architecture, *One:Twelve* is aimed at collecting the provocative ideas and intensities of the school's environment into a raw, dynamic platform of expression and analysis. Through the sharing of theories, experiences, and culture, *One:Twelve* becomes the voice of the students across physical and disciplinary boundaries, offering an intimate dialogue between local and even global communities.'

One:Twelve 3, Spring 2011; 95 × 147 mm; 24 pages; 500 copies

PABLO INTERNACIONAL MAGAZINE

Mexico City, Mexico;
London, UK
www.centrefortheaesthetic
revolution.blogspot.com

Pablo León de la Barra's zine
was launched in 2005 with
the tagline 'macho not rough:
art, men and architecture'.
The issues have consistently
brought together articles and
photography on architecture,
art and sexuality, with a focus
on Latin American culture.
Special editions are produced
to accompany exhibitions including a commission for the
2nd Trienal Poli/Gráfica de
San Juan: América Latina y el
Caribe. This issue uses photog
raphy to compare streets and
buildings in cities from Acapul
co and Bogotá to Los Angeles
and São Paulo.

Pablo Internacional Magazine: Paisaje Inútil / Useless Landscape /
Inútil Paisagem, 2010; 148 × 210 mm; 64 pages; 500 copies

P.E.A.R.

London, UK
www.pearmagazine.eu

An architectural zine presenting work from a variety of contemporary architectural practices, artists, researchers and individuals, *PEAR (Paper for Emerging Architectural Research)* aims to re-establish the fanzine as a primary medium for the dissemination of architectural ideas, musings, research and works. Through its presentation of a wide range of architectural discourses, *PEAR* seeks to present the complexity and variety of contemporary architectural practices. The zine was launched by editors Rashid Ali, Matthew Butcher, Julian Krueger and Megan O'Shea with designer Avni Patel in 2009.

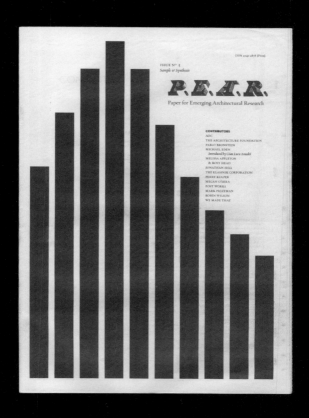

P.E.A.R. 3: Sample and Synthesis, May 2011; 289 × 400 mm; 47 pages; 1,000 copies

PIDGIN

Princeton, New Jersey, USA
www.pidgin-magazine.net

The student-run journal of the Princeton University School of Architecture was first published in 2006 by graduate students Marc McQuade, Caroline O'Donnell and Brian Tabolt to make the work generated at Princeton accessible to fellow students and the outside world.

Maintaining its 256-page format, *Pidgin* now operates with six student editors and features the work of students, faculty, staff and friends of the school. '*Pidgin* acts as both a language (pidgin) and a transmitter (pigeon) for the school. It's a marker of a moment in time, and an ongoing record of the school's interests.'

PIDGIN 10, April 2011; 170 × 240 mm; 256 pages; 1,000 copies

IKER GIL

ON RESEARCH, COLLABORATION AND DISCUSSION

Almost three years ago I decided to turn an idea that I had in my head into reality: to start a publication. A publication that could be created with the resources I had available (a laptop) and that could be produced at a faster pace than traditional methods of publishing allow.

Publishing has been an interest of mine for years although my training is strictly in architecture and I have always worked in what can be considered traditional architectural firms. My knowledge of the publishing world was strictly as a consumer, frequently acquiring both magazines and books, but no knowledge beyond that. Looking back at this interest, I think that there were two factors that determined my desire in starting a publication. The first one is my love for publications as objects themselves. I love a publication that is thoughtfully designed and carefully produced: one that knows how it wants to be experienced and is produced to achieve exactly that. Sometimes this requires an expensive production but at other times, a low-tech approach can be just as effective. The second factor is that I have always been interested in how other disciplines inform architecture. Through the lenses of not only photography, graphic design and industrial design but also sociology, economy and politics, I was able to identify other aspects of architecture that were as relevant as the ones covered by my own discipline. Whether you work at the scale of a piece of furniture, a building or a city, each project is the combination of a series of conditions, some related to design and some not. Looking at all these conditions with this kind of holistic approach has always been important to me.

When I decided to dedicate my time to establishing my own architectural practice I had a clear vision that the design work produced had to be paired with another arm that could become a tool for research, collaboration and discussion. An office that had my own voice as a designer but also facilitated the establishment of a platform for sharing the voice of others, whether architects or not, in order to instigate a fruitful discussion amongst the design community.

Andrew Clark and Andrew Dribin, colleagues with whom I had collaborated on a few projects, were interested in getting involved in the publication of a design journal and, with our resources and a small but enthusiastic team, we decided to put together a publication that would be released quarterly. Since then, we have published 11 issues dealing with topics such as Events, Work, Living, Energy, Amusement, Information, Public, Network, Conflict and most recently Speed. The publication is an ongoing project in itself, continuously refining its design, expanding the list of collaborators and understanding the potential audience. It became a non-profit organisation and, while the publication continues to be produced within the office, it exists as an independent entity. This decision was made to ensure that it was valued as an initiative on its own, without being mistakenly understood as just a PR effort for the practice. It is intended as a tool and a framework of discussion where ideas are valued without being compromised by prejudices of who produces or finances it.

IDENTIFIABLE BENEFITS

Producing a publication as part of an architecture office is not without challenges, such as coordinating the rigorous and fast-paced schedule of the publication with the deadlines of the projects in the office, or how to finance such an open-ended effort. However, we can begin to identify the benefits of producing a publication as part of the architectural practice: first, it is a fantastic excuse to research specific topics that we have some fascination for, and second, it facilitates collaboration with people from other perspectives and disciplines as a method of working.

In terms of research, the publication is a defined outcome that helps concentrate your efforts in a single topic in an organised and timely manner. You have a format and a schedule that does not vary from issue to issue, allowing you to focus on the content itself, whether that is in the format of a project, written or photographic essay, data visualisation or interviews. The topic of each issue reflects the current themes that affect the architectural discipline, but also themes that reflect the interests of the studio and the collaborating editors. In fact, it is common for the design work in the studio and research for the magazine to be combined. While these two areas remain clearly identifiable and separate, they continually influence and inform each other.

The architecture office in itself is closer to a flexible network of people that comes together for specific projects than a static hierarchical organization. This has been applied to all sorts of design projects and, most recently, a collaboration with photographer Andreas EG Larsson to document the units and residents of the Bertrand Goldberg-designed complex in Chicago. While it is a photographic project in its outcome, it was approached from an architectural and sociological point of view, which makes this collaboration the only possible way to produce the project in a successful way. Urban research, in particular, benefits when it is approached from multiple perspectives, and this may lead to a combination of data visualisation, photographs and essays, and the collaboration with architects, urban designers, economists, filmmakers, residents and visitors. This was the approach to the city of Shanghai in our book *Shanghai Transforming*.

A PROFITABLE RELATIONSHIP

Of course, the relationship between architects and the production of their publications is not just recent. We have innumerable examples, from the 1903 *Das Andere* publication edited by Adolf Loos, *L'Esprit Nouveau* founded in 1920 by Le Corbusier and Cubist painter Amédée Ozenfant and *Domus* founded by Gio Ponti in 1928, to *Archigram* started in 1961, *Oppositions* founded by Peter Eisenman, Kenneth Frampton and Mario Gandelsonas in 1973 and *Circo* founded in 1993 by Luis M Mansilla, Luis Rojo and Emilio Tuñón, just to name a few. In Network, our 2011 spring issue, we published an interview with architectural historian and theorist Beatriz Colomina by Ethel Baraona Pohl and César Reyes from the Barcelona-based collective dpr-barcelona. Beatriz is the co-editor, with Craig Buckley, of the book *Clip, Stamp, Fold: The Radical Architecture of Little Magazines, 196X – 197X* and the curator of the travelling exhibition of the same title. In the interview, Colomina establishes that 'all of the modern architects were involved in one way or another with the publishing industry'.[1] She continues by saying that 'Le Corbusier used them [publications] to communicate ideas that were not only related to architecture, but to cities and history in the decade of the 1920s, architects built themselves through the magazines. After that, in the 60s, the idea is the same. The best known case is Archigram. They were a group of architects working on this magazine, yet there's not an Archigram office, they didn't even know themselves as Archigram in those years. Archigram is simply what they do, a magazine.'[2]

A NEW SET OF TOOLS

Nowadays, we have access to a new set of tools that can make the process of producing and sharing information easier than ever. We have software to quickly lay out magazines, the internet to connect with people around the world and share content, and print-on-demand services that make small print-runs more cost-effective.

As a result, ease of access to these tools has given a voice to people who may not previously have been able to share their point of view. The filters between the producer and its potential audience have been removed. Now each one of us has the possibility to select the content, control how it is produced, and share it through our own channels. The author, alone or with whomever he decides to work, becomes the editor, designer, publisher and distributor.

This condition differs extensively from more traditional architectural publishing, in which the publisher determines the content, process, timing, outcome and distribution. This works when an architectural office has an established audience and the publisher, more often than not, produces some form of 'safe' monograph. Publications about architecture are generally not cheap to produce, so the economics have to be clear for the publisher before committing to any production. But what about the younger architecture offices without a massive following? What about the emerging trends that need to be discussed but cannot fit within conventional formats? What about the topics that are present in architecture but are not considered mainstream? This is where the use of these new tools is crucial, as they help overcome the challenges of traditional publishing, providing a way of bringing new ideas and approaches to the architectural field.

A growing relationship between architectural offices and independent publishing has not only helped to share new ideas but has also helped to explore new forms of collaboration between practices and other disciplines. This in turn becomes part of the culture of the office, a way of working and approaching problems where barriers between disciplines get blurred. This notion of blurring also relates to the format of the publication itself: physical copies complement the digital versions and vice versa; new means of production are followed by new means of consumption; the immediacy of the digital world with the attention to detail of the printed one. This feeds back into practice and, as Javier Arbona points out in an article about blogging culture published in *MAS Context*, 'many are blogging while designing, and vice versa, blurring distinctions between spaces for theory, collaboration, entertainment, documentation and production'.[3]

In the end, content and collaboration are key. However it must not be forgotten that a publication, whether printed or digital, is only one of the possible outputs of the content. Exhibitions, lectures, panel discussions, tours, design charrettes, film festivals, podcasts, actions and an innumerable amount of other platforms are at the disposal of architects. A smart combination of all these outputs that features solid content and has a desire to understand problems from the various points of view involved will, in the end, advance the wider architectural field and the office itself.

NOTES

1. Beatriz Colomina, Ethel Baraona Pohl, César Reyes, 'From Xerography to HTML': *MAS Context*, Network, 14 March 2011, www.mascontext.com/9-network-spring-11/02-from-xerography-to-html, retrieved September 2011.

2. Ibid.

3. Javier Arbona, 'Spaces for Architectural Discourse and the Unceasing Labour of Blogging', *MAS Context*, Information, 1 September 2010, www.mascontext.com/issue07_information/spaces_architectural_discourse/text.html, retrieved September 2011.

PIN–UP

New York City, USA
www.pinupmagazine.org

PIN-UP is a bi-annual 'Magazine for Architectural Entertainment' launched by architect Felix Burrichter while he was working at a corporate architecture firm in New York City. Through interviews, essays and photography, *PIN-UP* features a mix of established and emerging architects, artists and designers from around the world. A 2010 residency at the MAK Center resulted in a special Los Angeles issue that celebrated the modern to the kitsch, and included commissions for new case study houses by four experimental architects. The scope of *PIN-UP* now extends beyond the publication itself to curating exhibitions and hosting events.

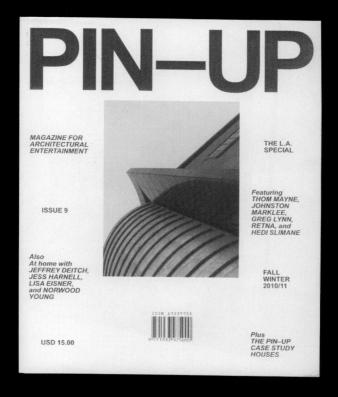

PIN–UP, Magazine for Architectural Entertainment 9,
Autumn / Winter 2010/11; 234 × 285 mm; 172 pages; 25,000 copies

PLAT

Houston, Texas, USA
www.platjournal.com

PLAT is a student-directed journal published out of the Rice School of Architecture. It aims to shift architectural discourse by stimulating new relationships between design, production and theory. Launched in 2010, *PLAT* operates by interweaving student, faculty and professional work into an open and evolving dialogue which progresses from issue to issue. Editors Seanna Walsh, Marti Gottsch and Erin Baer invite international submissions for the bi-annual issues to serve as a projective catalyst for architectural discourse.

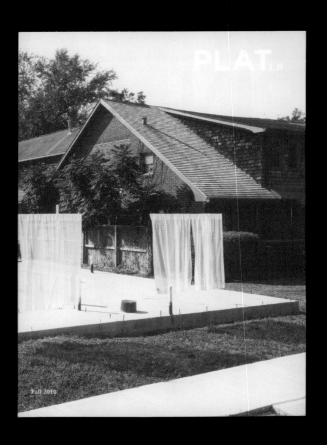

PLAT 1.0, Fall 2010; 160 × 222 mm; 152 pages; 1,000 copies

PLOT

Buenos Aires, Argentina
www.revistaplot.com.ar

PLOT is a platform for disseminating contemporary architectural practice and thinking. Launched in 2010 by a collective of architects and academics, the publication set out to offer new opportunities for architectural criticism and commentary from Latin America. '*PLOT* is idealistic. We are interested in discourse regarding the history, theory and criticism, technology, communications and science, aesthetics, social responsibility and politics.' After a year of publishing, issue 4 shows how *PLOT* has matured and defined its identity. 'Through feedback from architects, editors, friends and students, we are beginning to feel part of a big community. We are committed to represent different voices and to show Latin American production alongside the rest of the world.'

PLOT 4: Arriving Somewhere, June 2011; 232 × 297 mm; 240 pages; 7,000 copies

PRESTON IS MY PARIS

Preston / London, UK
www.prestonismyparis.
blogspot.com

Co-founded by Adam Murray and Robert Parkinson in June 2009, *Preston is my Paris* began as a photocopied zine focusing on the city of Preston but has since developed into a multi-faceted photographic archive consisting of 35 self-published works, live events and digital applications that address themes relating to everyday life, under-appreciated places, architecture and identity. *Preston Bus Sta-tion*, by Murray and Parkinson with Jamie Hawkesworth and Aidan Turner-Bishop, provides a document of a weekend spent in arguably Preston's most iconic building. 'By focusing on the users of the building and small architectural details, we aimed to produce an alternative to previous projects which tend to focus on the overall architectural structure. By appropriating the vernacular print format of news-print we were able to produce a photographic publication that was both affordable and acces-sible to all audiences.'

PRESTON BUS STATION

Preston Bus Station, October 2010; 290 × 380 mm; 12 pages; 500 copies

PUBLIC LIBRARY

Santiago, Chile;
www.publiclibrary.cl

Public Library is an independent
publishing house based in
Santiago, Chile, that publishes
the work of architects, artists,
photographers and designers.
It was founded in 2008 by architect Emilio Marin and graphic

designer Diego Córdova, and
joined by photographer Cristo-
bal Palma in 2010. The output
allows architects to experiment
with printed matter including
zines and posters. *Casa de Todos*
features a house designed by
Veronica Arcos in the foothills
of Santiago Chile.

Casa de Todos, October 2011; 148 × 210 mm; 124 pages; 100 copies

SAN ROCCO

Venice, Italy
www.sanrocco.info

San Rocco was launched in 2010 as 'a magazine about architecture' and takes its name from an unrealised competition entry by Giorgio Grassi and Aldo Rossi in 1971. The magazine, designed with a strong black-and-white identity, has a limited life of five years and will publish no more than 20 issues. The editors publish a call for papers for each issue and contributions can take the form of essays, illustrations, designs, comic strips or fiction. The second issue investigates the aesthetic consequences of the field, from both urban and architectural perspectives. Upcoming issues include *Scary Architects, 666 ways to be a communist architect* and *fuck concepts! context!* 'San Rocco is written by architects. As such, it is not particularly intelligent or philologically accurate.'

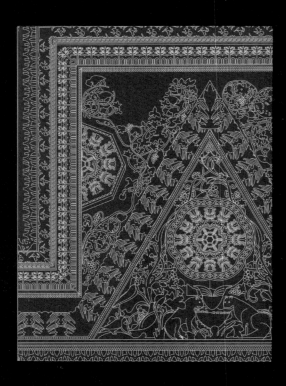

San Rocco 2: The Even Covering of the Field, Summer 2011
170 × 230 mm; 200 pages; 1,500 copies

SCAPEGOAT

Toronto, Canada
www.scapegoatjournal.org

Scapegoat, launched in 2010, examines the relationship between capitalism and the built environment, confronting the coercive and violent organisation of space, the exploitation of labour and resources, and the unequal distribution of environmental risks and benefits. 'As we witness the exacerbation of the latest global economic crisis, increasing demands for a programme of global austerity to "save capitalism", and the confrontations that arise from these intolerable conditions, architecture and landscape have been called on to manifest a new iconography for a collapsing civil society. *Scapegoat* responds: in the service of what future will our designs take form?'

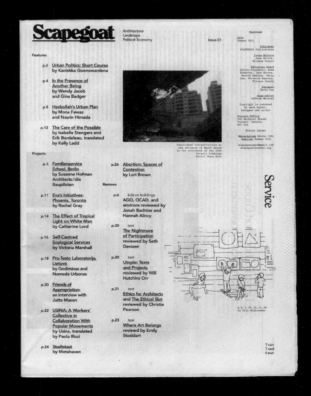

Scapegoat: Architecture | Landscape | Political Economy 1: Service, Summer 2011; 289 × 428 mm; 28 pages; 1,000 copies and online PDF

SCOPIO

Porto, Portugal
www.scopiomagazine.com

scopio magazine is a bi-annual publication on photography, architecture and public space from the Cityscopio Cultural Association and the Espaço F-FAUP / CCRE research group. The editors aim to promote awareness of the photographic image with regard to its ability to question real space and its experiences, a support and technique for the mediation and reception of architecture by a wider public, and an instrument for exploring spatial forms and new architecture. The publication, inspired by bookzines and taking its name from a Greek word describing an instrument for viewing, features visual narratives, texts or other related works in which photography is used as a research instrument. 'The intent is to present diverse visual narratives that convey a position, argument or story about a particular architectural problem.'

scopio 1$^{1/3}$: *Aboveground Architecture*, October 2010; 120 × 160 mm; 159 pages; 1,000 copies

SOILED

Chicago, USA
www.soiled.cartogram.org

Operating at the interstices of architecture, urbanism and the pedosphere, *SOILED* is a venue for dialogue and exploration. It investigates the role that the built environment plays in social issues of earthly but marginalised proportions; it documents hidden systems and in-between spaces. The editor-in-chief Joseph Altshuler and editorial team curate ideas, from the arable to the obscene, by seeking the active participation of multi-disciplinary contributors. *SOILED* employs narratives, manifestoes, mappings, ephemera and live events to mediate its architectural discourse to the broader public. By focusing on the surface of the skin as a natural mediator, *Skinscrapers* navigates a continuum of scale, starting inside the gut, proceeding to the contours of the body, and culminating in the anthropomorphic city. *SOILED* is published twice per year on each solstice.

SOILED 2: Skinscrapers, Summer 2011; 189 × 246 mm; 116 pages; print-on-demand and online PDF

SPAM_MAG

Santiago, Chile
www.spam.cl

SPAM magazine is focused on
being a tool of critical analysis
of the new spatial relationships
that are being generated and
their encounter with the social
and political changes of the
current city. *SPAM* is defined
by editor Pablo Brugnoli and
designer Kathryn Gillmore as
'an experimental course,
without precise destination of
the route, watching as a process
of experimentation, the move-
ment of the city, its services,
contacts and activities'. The
magazine seeks to create an
environment of open discussion,
without attempting to represent
and build an institutional policy.
It is committed to a vision
of multiplicity and diversity
with contributions from Chile
and abroad.

SPAM_mag, vol 6, June 2009; 170 x 220 mm; 94 pages; 2,000 copies

ADAM MURRAY

ON INSTRUMENTS FOR ENGAGEMENT

Cabins built in forests, clumsy blocks of painted-over graffiti, the bus station of England's newest city, rooftops in Seoul, cardboard houses, the office of a deceased relative, a personal celebration of post-industrial Sheffield, tennis courts, English transmission towers, houses covered in snow, a 40-year self-build in São Paulo. Diverse, instinctive and, at times, esoteric, these are some of the subjects that have been covered by a current group of photographers and artists who are offering a reappraised perspective on architecture and the built environment.

The built environment has consistently provided photographers with rich subject matter for work both in an artistic and commercial context. The pioneers of photography were able to take advantage of the static nature of buildings that allowed for the long set-up and exposure times that early technology dictated. Typologies produced by photographers such as Bernd and Hilla Becher and Donovan Wylie have encouraged audiences to focus on architectural form, the purpose of the buildings and what is considered worthy of such detailed photographic study. Architects rely on the pixel-perfect photograph to provide a document of their spectacular show-piece project before it is subjected to people actually using the construction. For many audiences, it is precisely this photograph that allows them at least some experience of a building that they will never gain access to.

Within both photography and the built environment there are long-standing hierarchical structures in terms of what is considered worthy of discussion and consequently, what discussion is

124

considered worthy. Often it is the grand or extraordinary architectural projects that are given the most discussion within relatively mainstream media, for example the Olympic facilities in London, the Beetham Tower in Manchester and the Park Hill Estate in Sheffield. These projects have the combination of spectacle, exoticism and public interest that will encourage a wide audience to read an article about them on their commute to work or over Sunday breakfast.

More in-depth debate is generally the realm of specialist publications and conferences that are contained within specific professional fields with the professional motivations that are inherent within these arenas. Trade journals such as *The Architects' Journal* and *Architect*, academic journals such as *The Journal of Architecture* and *Town Planning and Architecture*, and magazine-style publications such as *El Croquis* and *Detail*, all offer knowledgeable and informed debate to an audience that would consider themselves as peers of the writers and photographers featured.

The content of these publications has a clear emphasis on the written word. The role of photography within these publications is to inform and illustrate in that it gives a visual context to accompany the written article. This is not to undermine the work: each project has its own purpose and significant influence and can clearly be seen in many contemporary examples. However, through a project such as ARCHIIZNES it is possible to see that a new generation of photographers and artists believe that there is another role for photography in relation to the built environment and publishing practice. These practitioners are removing themselves from the mainstream professional press and are concerned with using photography as a visual language to critique and focus attention on the spaces that we occupy. This distance has allowed image-makers a new freedom in terms of the subject matter, aesthetic style and format that their work takes.

Looking through the selection of publications that is featured in the ARCHIZINES archive, only a few contain predominantly photography; the Belgian-based publication *UP* being one rare example. According to the editors, their work is focused on 'interesting architecture' and 'appears regularly with an irregular interval'. It is this subjective, idiosyncratic approach to architecture that makes their work stand out.

UP rebels against the mainstream architectural press in a number of ways; the format of the publication changes from stapled to concertina and there is a seemingly flexible identity for the group, but it is the subject matter and use of photography that is the distinguishing feature. This is a publication that turns its back on the latest mega-structure by celebrity architects, instead choosing to focus on subjects such as a house that Eduardo Longo began building in São Paulo in 1970 and is still unfinished, a Belgian architecture project from the mid 1950s and simply a series of doorways and corridors.

Text is kept to a minimum and the reader is left with work to do in terms of interpreting the meaning of the photographs. In one instance it begins seemingly as a relatively simple case of comparison between archive photographs of the house being built and how it stands now. But the question still remains, why this particular house? It is clearly unorthodox in terms of design and construction methods, but surely there must be other projects of this kind. As readers, we are then encouraged to consider how we would build our own house, and to ask ourselves whether projects like this are happening in our own towns and cities. The publication acts as a trigger for our imagination to dream about what is possible.

Issue 8 of *UP* moves further into the realms of conceptual documentary photography. There are some similarities to a typological study with repetitive composition and subject matter, but this is a project that uses photography and the physicality of print to deal with our interpretation and use of space. The concertina structure of the publication forces the reader to play with how the work is 'read'. Single pages can be looked at, but the real joy comes when the publication is stood up on a surface and an almost mirror-like juxtaposition occurs. This image relationship is changed, however, as the reader manipulates the pages, we are essentially involved in a basic version of an architect planning the structure of a building.

I started *Preston is my Paris* with Robert Parkinson in July 2009 in order to encourage the exploration of Preston in the northwest of England as a subject for creative practice and to generally focus more attention on the city. What originally started as a free zine and blog has developed into a multi-faceted project that includes exhibitions, digital applications and live events. Preston is my Paris Publishing was then set up to produce affordable, photography publications that focused attention on other places that are underappreciated aesthetically. Through the use of photography and appropriation of vernacular printing formats, we can explore how people perceive and experience their surroundings. Recent publications have focused on other cities, such as Derby and Carlisle.

Outside the realm of ARCHIZINES, there are many photographers producing one-off publications that use architecture and built space as a starting point. The work of Sheffield-based photographer Theo Simpson deals with subject matter that relates closely to his post-industrial hometown. His three self-published works, *Dead Ends*, *Eight* and *What We Buy*, feature discarded job centre slips, transmission towers and a range of products available to buy for £1 or less. It is possible to trace the subject of Simpson's work through the tradition of British documentary photography by people like John Davies, Paul Graham and Martin Parr, yet there could be no accusation of simple replication.

Although it could be argued that all of Simpson's work focuses on the built environment, his project *Eight* is clearly the most defined. This large-scale publication features a series of photographic screen prints of transmission towers. 'What fascinates me with transmission towers is that they are the second largest network of man-made structures in the UK, except you don't really notice them.' Simpson's intention instead is to focus on the 'intricacies and consideration of everyday structures'.

Beyond subject matter, Simpson's work really triumphs through the format in which it is presented. The publication is over half a metre in height and contains a series of loose screen prints, 'as I felt the graphic nature of the print method highlighted the lattice form of the structures'. In an era where digital technologies allow completed images of a structure to be produced even before it is physically finished, the tactile, individual and hand-crafted format encourages the reader to engage with and consider the subject matter that would normally be overlooked.

The role of an architect or town planner is to come up with an ideal to fulfill a particular purpose. The success of their solution is then communicated in the imagery used to show the work to a general audience. Buildings are photographed as spectacular beacons that often look more like computer-generated models rather than physical constructions. The press release for a redeveloped city centre is likely to be accompanied by photographs showing the streets and shops before the general public has been allowed in. The architects have done their job; this is the finished product, done.

But what happens when people actually start using the buildings? Although it does not necessarily fit in with the utopian plans of the initial project, a building is inert until people engage with it. Inevitably the built environment changes as people bring their own personal methods of use and values to the table. This study of the way people operate within the built environment has increasingly become the focus of photographic projects.

Produced in a photocopied, zine-like format, photographer Chris Seddon released 50 copies of his publication *Correctionism*. This is a photographic documentation of the deletion of graffiti that has been put on to public space in Hackney and Tower Hamlets. This is the opposite of the ideal visions that commissioned architectural photography would normally like to portray; this is what happens when people become involved.

The initial graffiti is put there by someone wanting to impose his or her identity on a particular environment; other people who also engage with that environment may not like this and it has been decided that the role of the council responsible for this area is to delete or 'correct' this work by painting over the graffiti. Consequently this leaves an obvious paint mark on the area and this has been interpreted by Seddon as being a different form of graffiti. Although graffiti is often the subject of terribly clichéd and repetitive work, this photographic project offers a new perspective. It is about the ideals that people have with regard to public space and the built environment and about who possesses the power to impose these ideals.

Released as a self-published photobook in 1999, *Dad's Office* by Nigel Shafran also shows how something that at first could be seen as having only personal interest actually addresses universal themes. It is the ambiguous nature of the subject matter that makes this work focused on a building particularly engaging. There are mixed signs as to what it is that we are looking at: the title suggests it is the work environment of the author's father, but the different rooms featured correlate more with our understanding of domestic rather than work space. The glimpses of trees and houses that we see out of the window reinforce this idea of suburbia.

In the same way that *Correctionism* makes us question the purpose and role of the cities that we inhabit, *Dad's Office* uses deeply personal subject matter to make the reader question the purpose and role of the spaces around us. Objects such as the desk, rusty stapler and phone book suggest a work space, but the ironing board, wine glasses and toothache medicine contradict this. Although an architect may initially have determined a building to be either home or office, this publication encourages the reader to consider why this purpose should be fixed.

IANN is a bi-annual contemporary art photography magazine published simultaneously in Korea and Japan. In September 2009 an issue was released with the title Nameless Cities. Featuring mainly photographic work from a range of practitioners including Chikashi Suzuki, Paul Graham, Yoon-Jean Lee and Niels Stomps, the publication aims to offer different visual interpretations of urban spaces.

One of the less instantly spectacular of the projects featured in the publication is called *rooftops, Seoul* by Jan Lemitz. Understated in aesthetic style and taking up just four pages of the publication, it relates very much to the idea of how people engage with urban space. The space in this case is not public space or an iconic building, but simply the rooftops of a series of buildings in Seoul.

Flat and with balcony-style walls, you would be unable to see these rooftops from the street and they do not have the instant aesthetic seduction values that other buildings in Seoul must have. The uniform composition of the photographs encourages analysis and comparison. Some of the rooftops are in a state of disrepair; others seem to have been turned into garden-like areas for a family to use. Although interesting in terms of offering a viewpoint into spaces not normally seen, the real success of this project is that Lemitz raises issues to do with how space is used within the modern city and the value of this space in a way that does not seek to impose opinion.

With the amount of valuable and relevant work that is currently being produced, it would be a challenge to produce a comprehensive survey. What the work discussed in this essay aims to highlight is the variety of approaches in terms of subject matter, aesthetic style and treatment of the printed outcome. An appropriate summation of this body of work would be the concept of being informed by 'real users' and the importance of this should not be underestimated. By questioning the role that photography has in relation to architecture and the built environment, practitioners and audiences are being provoked into actively engaging with subjects that are relevant to them. Using photography as the language of communication then enables a different group of people to contribute their opinion and understanding to the wider debate.

THRESHOLDS

Cambridge, Massachusetts, USA
thresholds.mit.edu

Thresholds is a journal edited by students at the MIT Department of Architecture. Reflecting the department's interdisciplinary nature with foci in architecture, art, design, urbanism, history and technology, *Thresholds* publishes scholarly and project-based work that revolves around an independent theme chosen for each issue. Topics covered in the Future issue include anti-Taylorisation art, golf landscapes and the history of Lenin's dead body. Originally launched in 1992 as a curated collection of essays and projects, *Thresholds* was relaunched in its current format as an annual peer-reviewed journal in 2009.

Thresholds 38: Future, February 2011; 200 × 230 mm; 96 pages; 1,000 copies

TOO MUCH

Tokyo, Japan
www.toomuchmagazine.com

TOO MUCH, a magazine about 'romantic geography', is produced by international writers and photographers with a Japanese design team. As the world enters an era of widespread urbanisation, *TOO MUCH* gathers thoughts about cities, the people who live in them and the effects they have on societies and our environment. The magazine also reports on migrations in and between cities, and the impact this has on race, nationality, language, tradition and customs. Issue 2 of *TOO MUCH* – as a response to the recent catastrophic earthquake in Japan – looks at experiences related to rebuilding, relocating, shelter building and the construction of ideal cities.

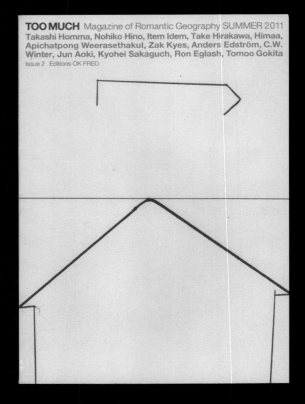

TOO MUCH: Magazine of Romantic Geography 2, July 2011
182 × 257 mm; 100 pages; 10,000 copies

TOUCHING ON ARCHITECTURE

London, UK
www.i-cabin.co.uk

Touching on Architecture is published by i-cabin(texts), the publishing department of the social, architectural and artistic research project i-cabin. The sporadic series of saddle-stitched booklets is a step into architecture via the critical work of a single non-architect. Writers, artists, musicians, designers and theorists are invited to publish their current work or research, in reflection of how these outputs touch upon architectural constructions. The first issue presents illustrators and graphic designers The Jan Press' perspective on the role of architecture in society.

Touching on Architecture 1: Touching Architecture by The Jan Press, 2008; 148 × 210 mm; 34 pages; 50 copies

UP

Antwerp / Brussels, Belgium

UP is a fanzine about 'interesting architectures' published by artists Koenraad Dedobbeleer and Kris Kimpe. Each issue is presented in A5, stapled or concertina folded, and features photography by Dedobbeleer, Kimpe and others of a single work of architecture that inspires them. A simple text provides credit and dates for the architect and photographer. Issue 8 reads: 'The issue stars the "door situation" of the master bedrooms at Haus Lange in Krefeld, designed by Mies van der Rohe in 1928. Photographs were taken in January 2009 by Volker Döhne.'

UP 8, August 2009; 148 × 210 mm; 10 pages; 1,500 copies

UR

Buenos Aires, Argentina
www.ur-arquitectura.com.ar

Conceived by Ariel Jacubovich, Sofía Picozzi and Florencia Alvarez, *UR* attempts to expand the discourse and the possibilities of architecture by making visible certain contemporary points of view and forms of production that intersect in Buenos Aires. 'It is a collection of projects, works and processes which, when grouped together, give rise to a new reading.' Themed issues in English and Spanish connect projects and the people who participate in them to broader cultural issues. Launched in 2006, the editorial team is currently considering its future direction.

UR 2: Conversar / Conversing, November 2007
170 × 230 mm; 176 pages; 2,000 copies

VOLUME

Amsterdam, Netherlands
www.volumeproject.org

Launched in 2005, *VOLUME* is 'an independent quarterly magazine that sets the agenda for architecture and design'. It is produced as a collaboration between *Archis* (Arjen Ooster-man, Lilet Breddels, Jeroen Beekmans, Joop de Boer, Timo-thy Moore, Vincent Schipper), AMO (Rem Koolhaas, Reinier de Graaf), C-Lab (Jeffrey Inaba, Benedict Clouette) and other external partners. 'By going beyond architecture's defini-tion of "making buildings" it reaches out for global views on designing environments, advo-cates broader attitudes to social structures and reclaims the cul-tural and political significance of architecture. Created as a global ideas platform to voice archi-tecture any way, anywhere, any-time, it represents the expansion of architectural territories and the new mandate for design.' *VOLUME* was created as a continuation of *Archis* magazine which launched in 1986, which again is a continuation of *Wonen / TABK*, formed in turn from two magazines dating from 1946 and 1929.

VOLUME 28: Internet of Things, July 2011
276 × 200 mm; 176 pages plus insert; 5,100 copies

THE WEATHER RING

Perth, Australia
www.theweatherring.
wordpress.com

The Weather Ring is a journal that explores architecture and design in Western Australia. It was launched by Andrew Murray and Clare Wohlnick out of an interest in the uncharted histories, stories and work from the state: 'Through our investigations we hope to contribute to the understanding of our design history. We feel the fourth issue is moving closer to what we aimed for when we began the magazine. It contains new work by practices that have rarely been published, and interviews with designers involved with projects we feel need to be discussed. It also has the best jokes on the cover.'

The Weather Ring 4, February 2011; 210 × 297 mm;
40 pages with A3 insert; 200 copies and online PDF

WHAT ABOUT IT?

Beijing, China
www.wai-architecture.com

What About It?, aka a *'WAIzine'*, is a 'graphic narrative in magazine format' that presents the ideas, projects and research from WAI Architecture Think Tank's Nathalie Frankowski and Cruz Garcia, currently based in Beijing. It is aimed to serve as a platform through which questions are asked, ideas are diffused, and discussions are initiated. *What About It?* includes critical and theoretical texts, research projects, narrative architectures and architectural and urban experiments that have been developed by WAI.

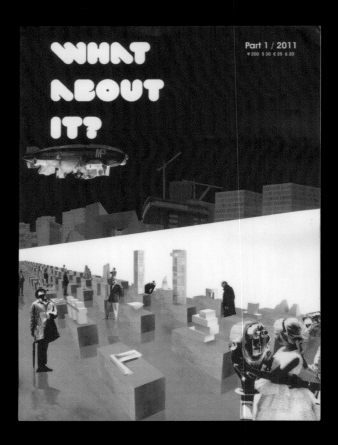

What About It? Part 1, February 2011; 210 × 297 mm; 100 pages; 50 copies plus online

MATTHEW CLARKE, ANG LI
& MATTHEW STORRIE

ON A WORD:

OBJECT!
OBJECT!
OBJECT!

To educate is to discuss, but with a bit of publishing energy, words spread. Whose words, words owed to whom and the patrons of words are factors that not only influence editorial decision-making, but those that predetermine their content. While academic publishing is not exempt from these factors, it lends itself to a degree of experimentation disallowed by the economies of store-shelf design magazines. Although no journal is truly independent, the most interesting academic work is being published by those who understand that when words spread, their meanings change. The tension emerging out of these discordant definitions sets a stage for academic architectural publishing. So in the spirit of alternative definitions, we offer a single word that continues to polarise the world of academic publishing. We can only speak from our editorial perspective, but we would like to believe the following is true everywhere:

Objectives are often too heavy.
To object is healthy.
The object is fine.

OBJECT AS AGENDA

The goal or end of an activity or effort

Agendas carry political and editorial persuasions; and while school journals aren't agenda-less, editors often intend to provide a neutral carrier of a school's myriad fascinations, fetishes and follies. On the outside, journals mark and record a school's evolving interests, but from within, they calibrate a school's interests with the larger architectural community. A successful publication brings both to the same table. As both a documentary record and a critical voice of the student body, student journals oscillate between introspection and outward declaration.

Whether or not editors confess to an agenda, changes in discourse require the agenda to remain flexible. This flexibility comes not without criticism. Given the informal nature of many editorial boards and the freedom from administrative oversight (for some), student editors grapple with this lack of agenda – should they publish thematic issues? Should they bring outside perspectives into the school? Should they curate contemporary themes? Many respond by acknowledging neutrality as an asset – a badge of independence and freedom from disciplinary baggage.

One former critic at Princeton University commented on this 'ruthlessly explicit' neutrality; why couldn't the visibility of student publications serve to curate a culture of the school and at the same time, to challenge this culture by bringing content to the inside? Editors of student publications confront this with every issue, having to reconcile the bird's-eye perspective of editor while also encouraging contributors to submit highly personal pieces. While some journals work through this with themed issues, others utilise the rapid turnover of editors to maintain currency in a changing architectural community. The more independence the editors have from their sponsors, the easier this is to accomplish. Independence, however, is not always an option, and in order to maintain a critical standard, student editors must find more oblique tactics.

As a result of this political structure, many focus on marginalised discourses, projects and ideas not foregrounded in studio projects or dissertations, but that arise naturally out of the academic community. Perhaps it's even the fashionable thing to do. Digital processes, obscure histories, personal hobbies and travelogues are common topics. While some could argue that these will be outweighed by grander narratives, we like to think that voices from the margins are louder than they seem. It is the task of student journals to advance these voices.

There has never been a grand narrative, epic history or complete story that accounted for all contradictory positions. Not only would this be a preposterous demand, but it would be too absolute. Too deterministic. Too self-important. Too aggrandising. Perhaps more appropriate for architectural anthologies, the big picture is unlikely to appear in contemporary journals.

As that same critic mentioned, some academic publications are the equivalent of taking a snapshot of everyone's hard-drive, a record of unfinished ideas. We contend that incompletion is not equal to invalidation. Without strict peer-review or the demands of an external publisher, journals remain a nimble and contemporary platform for an interface between academia and the larger architectural world. At the same time, editors undergird this noise with a consistent format, standards of quality and a vision for composition. In the best senses, academic journals serve to validate these margins.

OBJECT AS CONTENT

Something mental or physical toward which thought, feeling, or action is directed

If architectural anthologies solidify shifts in central discourse, academic journals leverage marginal discussions by being much more liquid (not necessarily slippery or soft). They fill the gaps between conflicting modes of practice, histories and theories. Academic journals may not turn over the rocks of history, but they are always the pebble in your shoe. They tease, annoy, agitate and provoke until you stop to make the proper adjustments. If students value this position for its historical value, it is crucial that their words maintain a balance between active opposition and passive recording.

Journals can exchange ideas at the speed of desk critiques or juried reviews, offering stages for multiple, agile performers. While this is an advantage to those valuing flexibility, it is hostile to agendas seeking 'comprehensive' knowledge. Unlike the broad swaths painted across history by figures such as Semper, Riegl and Giedion, journals remain agile to respond to a changing discipline. Although absolute histories offer model methodologies as well as comprehensive narratives, they require a broader contextualisation than available in the current journal format.

The advantage of quick exchange is that many architects – students, faculty, practitioners, historians and theorists alike – can be involved in a single project. Even as a project gains support through publication and citations – a measure of clout that Dave Hickey calls 'social value' – the focus may be elevated to a higher level of scrutiny. Many in the scientific community measure this kind of influence using Jorge Hirsch's h-index, a ranking of an author's influence based on the number of citations he/she receives. Using such quantifiable rankings, however, may not be so beneficial to the architectural community: as of September 2011, Google Scholar shows that Giedion has had 4,012 published citations. By this metric, Giedion is slightly more important than Riegl and Semper combined (touting 2,210 and 1,123, respectively). By the same meaningless measure, alternative publications should be considered useless simply because they have yet to be indexed by the primary academic indexes.

Editors who embrace this impermanence escape the scrutiny surrounding an inconsistent agenda. What's wrong with a well-lubricated conversation? What's wrong with a short-term memory? We say 'nothing', but we deny the influence of Nietzsche or Giedion; amnesia in the digital age is of the attention-deficit kind. Whether by design or accident, the more informal academic journals have reversed roles with the fleeting internet media. Low print-runs and limited internet visibility ensure that academic journals are easy to read, ingest and *forget*. Ironically, searchable text, pirated copies and internet archives have made online publications the more permanent option.

Debate sparks tension, and when it occurs without rest, it can breed deeply seated grudges. Although architectural debates have long taken place in academic journals, the digital context forces some informality into the battleground; likely opponents know the opposition may not last long. As it stands, informal academic publications can provide the spectacle without the collateral damage.

OBJECT AS MATERIALITY

Something material that may be perceived by the senses

The ubiquity of digital publications has given birth to the notion of amorphous content, no longer bound by the margins of the page. In a culture of speedy reproductions, standardised formats are stripped of their authority, and publications can no longer be pegged by their covers. Content, in turn, is presented with an eviction notice, and is forced to trade in its permanent address for a life on the road.

In light of this, architectural publications must think of their containers as metaphorical camper vans, with a large turnover of passengers. As vehicles for recording and distributing particular moments within schools, content remains in transience, while the exterior becomes a fetish object within the cult of the immaterial. While each favours its own format – from a stapled pamphlet to bound magazine – *Pidgin* publishes with a less frequent, object-like book.

As both current documents and historical objects, journals are painfully aware of their containers. Some are too large for the scanner or the photocopier. Some are too small. Some politely interrupt the status-quo of the bookshelf. Some fit snugly into your coat pocket and others are more forgiving of a tight roll before being discarded. Regardless of the action, printed journals force their readers to engage with their physiques, and the act of reading becomes inevitably linked to their mass. It's the only proper difference between a light and heavy read.

The presence of journals as a tangible object is by no means auxiliary. Editorial decisions are intertwined with choices around typography, paper weight and size, whereby content is repeatedly sifted through the filter that is format. However, journals should by no means be precious about their own physicality. While they participate within larger discussions around the need for the enduring within a disposable digital culture, collectability has less to do with a nostalgic longing for printed matter than a desire to present itself as an architectural product. Most of the time, journals consist of paper and ink, but every once in a while, they could just as easily be a solid tablet.

By escaping the institutionalised space of the bookshelf, journals should embrace their physicality and their potentials as multi-functional components. They should willingly assume the role of doorstop or paperweight without the slightest hesitation. After all, academic journals cannot assume they will be read in the solitary reading environment of St Jerome's study. They are dispatches, social agents, conversation starters. They demand to be picked up spontaneously, carried from place to place with an air of casual abandon, or passed around amongst acquaintances.

Please spread the word.

CONTRIBUTORS

Matthew Clarke, Ang Li and Matthew Storrie
are editors of *Pidgin* and graduate students of the
Princeton University School of Architecture.

Pedro Gadanho is an architect, curator and writer
based in Lisbon. He has an MA in art & architecture and holds a PhD in architecture & mass-
media from FAUP, where he currently teaches.
He is also a guest teacher at BIARCH and ESA.
He curated several events and exhibitions, including 'Metaflux', the Portuguese representation at
the 2004 Venice Architecture Biennale, and 'Space
Invaders', for the British Council. His designs
include the Orange and GMG houses. He writes
in shrapnelcontemporary.wordpress.com.

Iker Gil is an architect, urban designer and director of MAS Studio. In addition he is the editor
in chief of *MAS Context* and an adjunct assistant
professor at the School of Architecture at UIC.
He is the recipient of the 2010 Emerging Visions
Award from the Chicago Architectural Club.

Adam Murray is a lecturer on the Photography
course at the University of Central Lancashire,
a photographer and co-founder of *Preston is my
Paris*. Murray's work focuses on subjects relating
to everyday life and has been featured in a number
of publications including *Photoworks, British
Journal of Photography, Art Review* and *Le Monde*.

Elias Redstone is an independent curator, writer and consultant. He is the founder and curator of ARCHIZINES, the editor-in-chief of the *London Architecture Diary* and an online columnist for the New York Times' *T Magazine*. Previously, he curated the Polish Pavilion at the 2010 Venice Architecture Biennale and was senior curator at the Architecture Foundation.

Rob Wilson is a curator, architect and editor of *Block* magazine. His most recent exhibition was 'Facade: Through a Glass Darkly' at the National Glass Centre, Sunderland, and he is curating an exhibition on colour in architecture at the V&A in 2012. He has written for magazines including *Blueprint, Archis, Kunstforum, Tate Etc* and *The Architectural Review*. Previously curator of exhibitions at the RIBA, he is an associate lecturer in Criticism, Curation and Communication at Central St Martins.

Mimi Zeiger is editor and publisher of *loud paper*, a zine and blog dedicated to increasing the volume of architectural discourse, and *Maximum Maxim MMX*. As a writer and critic, she covers art, architecture and design for a number of publications including *The New York Time*s, *Domus, Dwell* and *Architect*, where she is a contributing editor. Zeiger is author of *Tiny Houses* and *Micro Green: Tiny Houses in Nature*. Always obsessed with the intersection of architecture and media, she is director of communications at Woodbury School of Architecture.

ACKNOWLEDGEMENTS

Elias Redstone wishes to thank all the editors whose publications are the subject of ARCHIZINES; Wayne Daly and Zak Kyes at Bedford Press; Brett Steele, Vanessa Norwood, Lee Regan, Luke Currall and Sue Barr at the AA; Albert Folch and Diego Córdova at Folch Studio; and Simon Fujiwara, Sarah Ichioka, Catherine Ince, Justin Jaeckle, Donna Loveday, Erin Manns, Catherine McDermott, Sophie O'Brien, Vicky Richardson and Debbie Whitfield for their ongoing support, encouragement and enthusiasm for the ARCHIZINES project.

A special thank you to Sebastian Coles; and to Marc Ward, Elizabeth James and Abraham Thomas for their role in providing a permanent home for the ARCHIZINES collection in the National Art Library at the V&A.

COLOPHON

ARCHIZINES
Edited by Elias Redstone
Published by Bedford Press

Copy editor: Clare Barrett
Design: Bedford Press
Design assistant: Laurie Robbins
Archizines logo: Folch Studio
Printed in Germany by
GGP Media GmbH, Pössneck

ISBN 978-1-907414-20-6

Bedford Press, AA Publications Ltd
36 Bedford Square, London WC1B 3ES

www.bedfordpress.org

Bedford Press is an imprint of AA Publications Ltd, which is a wholly owned subsidiary of the Architectural Assciation (Inc) Registered Charity No 311083. Company limited by guarantee. Registered in England No 171402. Registered office as above.

Published on the occasion of ARCHIZINES exhibition at the Architectural Association School of Architecture, 5 November – 14 December 2011